The Spider Web

The Spider Web

Royal Navy Air Service
Flying Boat Operations
During the First World War
by a Flight Commander

P. I. X.

(Theodore Douglas Hallam)

LEONAUR

*The Spider Web: Royal Navy Air Service Flying Boat Operations
During the First World War by a Flight Commander*
by P. I. X. (Theodore Douglas Hallam)

Leonaur is an imprint of Oakpast Ltd

ISBN: 978-1-84677-784-4 (hardcover)
ISBN: 978-1-84677-783-7 (softcover)

http://www.leonaur.com

Publisher's Notes

The views expressed in this book are not necessarily
those of the publisher.

Contents

Dedication

To the jolly fine fellows, officers and men,
of the war flight, Felixstowe.

My acknowledgments are due to the editor of *Blackwood's Magazine* and to the editor of *The Times*.

P. I. X.

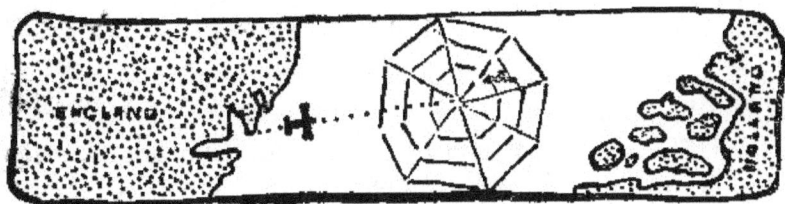

CHAPTER 1

The Spider Web

ONE

There is magic in salt water which transmogrifies all things it touches. The aeroplane with its cubist outline undergoes a sea change on reaching the coast and becomes a flying-boat, a thing of beauty, a Viking dragon ship, a shape born of the sea and air with pleasant and easy lines, and in the sun, the dull war-paint stripped from the natural mahogany, a flashing golden craft of enchantment.

During the war nothing was published about the flying-boats, partly because they worked with the Silent Navy, and partly because they were produced in the service. They were created to harry and destroy the German submarines, and were a manifestation of the genius of the English-speaking peoples for all things connected with the sea.

There is a tang of salt in the adventures of the men who boomed out in them over the narrow waters, for they had to do with submarines and ships, and all that that implies. In their job o'work of bombing U-boats, attacking Zeppelins, fighting enemy seaplanes, and carrying out reconnaissance and convoy duties, there is as much romance as in any particular effort in the war. In the future, grown great in size, the boats will form the winged Navy, and will carry mails and passengers over the water-routes of all the world.

Boat seaplanes, or flying-boats as they are called by the men who use them, are a true type of aircraft designed for dealing with the chances and hazards of flying over the sea. They have a stout wooden boat hull, planked with mahogany and cedar, to which the wings, with the engines between the planes, are attached. They carried a service crew of four: Captain, navigator, wireless operator, and engineer. Float seaplanes, which the boats superseded, were practically land-machines with two wooden floats instead of wheels, and struck you as being aeroplanes on a visit to the seaside which had put on huge galoshes in order to keep dry. On seeing one pass overhead it was usual to say: "There she goes with her big boots on."

Float seaplanes were not very seaworthy, breaking up quickly in rough water; and many a brave lad, down at sea in them with engine trouble, has been drowned. They are very much today what they were in 1914.

From the very beginning of things there was much faith shown by the sea-going pilots of the Royal Naval Air Service in the seaplane as a weapon to do down the U-boat. But the technical people of the service neglected float seaplanes; and flying-boats, of which they did not approve, took a long time to develop. Instead of perfecting seaplanes the slide-rule merchants developed scout land machines with the idea of using them off the decks of ships, and a strong force of aeroplane pilots was collected and provided with fast and handy aeroplanes. The Navy was not ready to use this force, only being converted to its value in 1918, and it was sent to assist the Royal Flying Corps, when the latter was in difficulties in France owing to the lack of pilots and efficient machines. Unfortunately this effort turned a great deal of the energy of the R.N.A.S. away from seaplanes and anti-submarine work.

There would probably not have been any big British flying-

PORTE BABY WITH BRISTOL BULLET ON TOP PLANE

boats but for the vision, persistence, and energy, in the face of disbelief and discouragement, of Colonel J. C. Porte, C.M.G., who designed and built at Felixstowe Air Station the experimental machine of each type of British flying-boat successfully used in the service. His boats were very large, the types used in the war weighing from four and a half to six and a half tons, and carried sufficient petrol for work far out from land and big enough bombs to damage or destroy a submarine other than by a direct hit. The pilots were out in the bow of the boat, with the engines behind them, and so had a clear view downward and forward. The boats were very seaworthy, and no lives were lost in operations from England owing to unseaworthiness.

In designing and perfecting flying-boats there were more difficulties than in producing float seaplanes, for the technical problems were great, while engines of sufficient horsepower were not to be had in the early part of the war, and indifference and scepticism had to be overcome. It was not until the spring of 1917 that suitable flying-boats were in being. But this was in time for them to meet the big German submarine effort, when the great yards at Weser, Danzig, Hamburg, Vagesack, Kiel, and Bremen, working day and night, with production driven to its highest pitch by standardisation, were pouring out into the North Sea an incredible number of U-boats.

During this year a year when it looked as though the Undersea boats would strangle our merchant shipping and the danger was greater to England than her people realised forty flying-boats were put into commission, and sighted sixty-eight enemy submarines and bombed forty-four of them.

A submarine is a steel boat shaped something like a cigar. When on the surface it is driven by two petrol engines. Under the surface it is driven by two electric motors, the electricity being obtained from storage batteries. At the bow and stern are horizontal rudders known as hydroplanes. Under ordinary circumstances, when the submarine is about to dive, water is let into tanks until the boat is just floating on the surface with only the conning-tower showing. The petrol engines are stopped and

12

the electric motors are started. Then the hydroplanes are turned down and they force the submarine under the water. The submarine uses its power of travelling under the water to stalk its prey and to hide from its enemies.

When the intensive German submarine campaign began, the methods of hunting U-boats from surface ships had not been perfected. The hydrophone was crude, the technique of using depth charges was not perfected, and the mines and nets were not adequate. Also, the Dover barrage was not then in being. So Fritz, as the service called the Hun submarine, went south-about from his bases to his hunting-grounds.

Picture the sinister grey steel tubes dropping away from the dock in the German harbour as the Commander in the conning-tower gave the order to cast off, the swirl of water at the stern as the twin propellers took up their job, and the gay flutter of signal flags hoisted to the collapsible mast as they passed out of the harbour a harbour which they would not see, if all went well with them, for from fifteen to twenty-five days, and which, if things went well for the Allies, they would never see again. Once outside the harbour, the Commander would order the engines whacked up to the economical cruising speed of eight to nine knots, a speed at which he could do about two hundred miles a day, and would then turn south, and so proceed on the surface through the North Sea to the Straits of Dover.

Passing through the Straits, either at night on the surface or in the daytime under the water, the Commander would pass down the south coast of England and cruise on the surface in the chops of the English Channel or off the approaches to Ireland. Here he would meet our merchant ships coming in with food, raw material, munitions, and passengers, and either sink them by gunfire or by torpedo. The attack would be made without warning. Sometimes survivors, who had got away in boats from the doomed vessel, would be shelled. And once the survivors were taken on the deck of a submarine, their lifebelts removed, and then the submarine submerged, leaving the unfortunates to drown.

On their run through the North Sea the submarines passed between the Hook of Holland and Harwich Harbour, the distance between the two places being one hundred miles.

Harwich Harbour is a sheltered stretch of water on the East Coast made by the rivers Stour and Orwell emptying into the southern portion of the North Sea. It was the centre of intense anti-Hun activity. It was here that Rear-Admiral Tyrwhitt had his "hot-stuff" destroyer flotilla, that the hydrophone for detecting enemy submarines under the surface of the sea was evolved, that our own submarines which operated in the Bight of Heligoland had their base, and where the flying-boat station of Felixstowe was situated. And it was at Felixstowe that the service experimental flying-boats were designed and built, and a flying-boat squadron operated. During 1917 this squadron, which used an average of only eight boats a month, sighted forty-seven enemy submarines and bombed twenty-five, besides destroying enemy seaplanes and bringing down a Zeppelin in flames.

It was my good fortune to be posted to Felixstowe Air Station in March 1917 and to be put in charge of the flying-boat operations. So this is a yarn about the beginnings and work of a single flying-boat station, but it is characteristic of the work carried out at the seaplane stations strung along the South and East Coasts of Great Britain, from the Scilly Islands, off Land's End, to the Orkneys and Shetlands, off the north of Scotland. If the names and deeds of the pilots at Felixstowe are alone recorded, it is not that equally gallant and skilful men were not harrying the Hun elsewhere, but that their adventures would fill many volumes.

Two

In the curious quirks of fortune and chance which moved people across oceans and continents to play their part in the war, and finally fetched them up, in some cases, in the jobs which they most desired to fill, there are all the elements of romance. Just before the war broke out I was occupying a room at the "Aviator's Home," a boarding-house in the small American in-

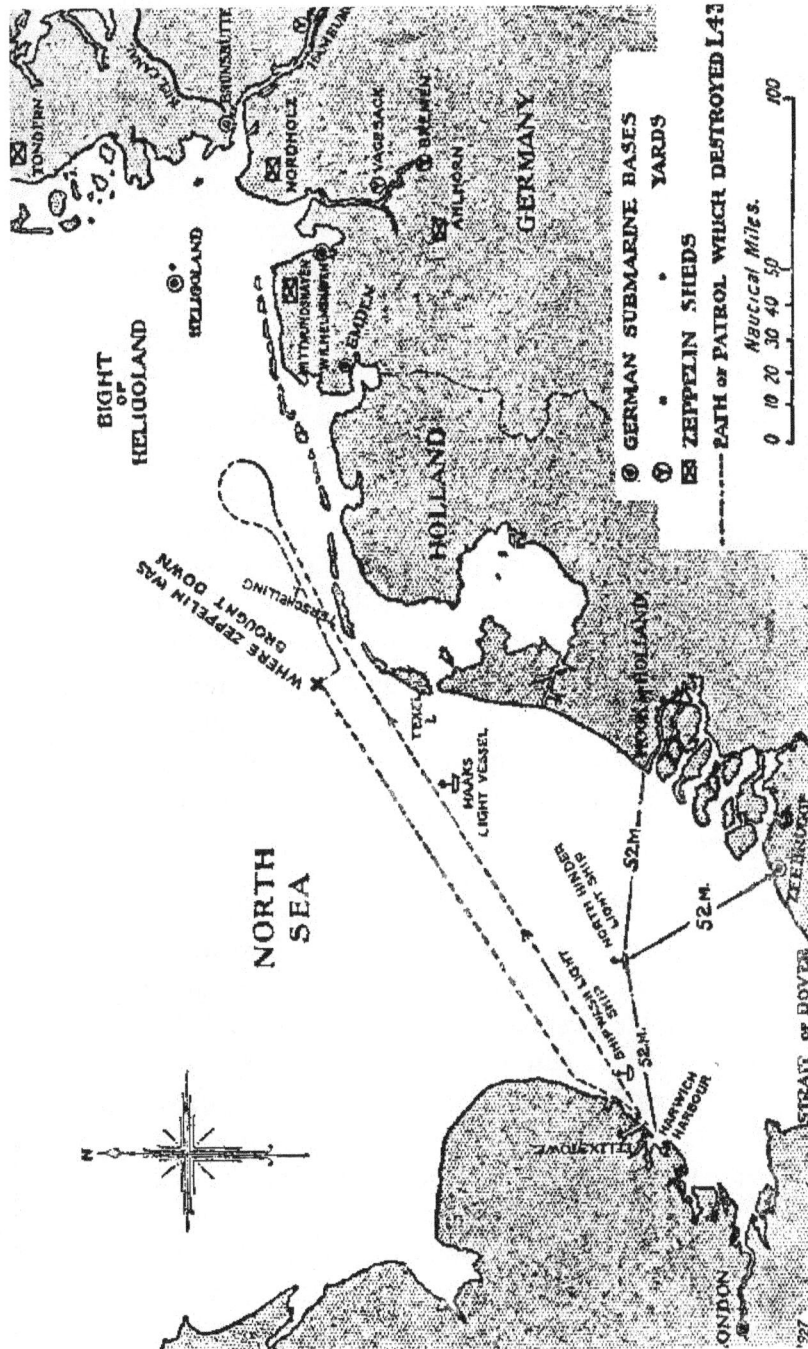

CHART SHOWING THE SOUTHERN PORTION OF THE NORTH SEA AND THE BIGHT OF HELIGOLAND

land town of Hammondsport, N.Y. This town was situated on a long narrow lake, with a forked end, a lake surrounded by steeply rising vine-clad hills to which clung the white wooden houses of the vine-growers, and in which were dug the huge cellars for storing the excellent champagne of the district.

It was here that Mr Glen Curtiss built his flying-boats before the war, having recruited his labour at first from the ranks of the local blacksmiths, carpenters, and young men with a mechanical turn of mind. And it was here that I first tasted the smoke of a Fatima cigarette, a particularly biting smoke affected by Yankee airmen, and went out in a flying-boat for the first time in July 1914. This boat, to memory quaint and medieval, had a single engine alleged to develop sixty horsepower; it belonged to the dim dark ages when compared to the latest boat I have flown, the eighteen hundred horsepower Felixstowe Fury.

Finishing the course of instruction a few days after the declaration of war, and receiving no satisfaction by cabling to the Admiralty and War Office offering my services as a pilot, which rather annoyed me at the time, but which I now know was probably due to their being somewhat preoccupied with other little matters, I returned to my home in Toronto, Canada, and joined the first Canadian contingent as a private in a machine-gun battery.

Arriving in England in the steerage of a troopship in October 1914, I satisfied at Lockyears in Plymouth a great hunger and thirst, bred of army fare and a dry canteen, with a most delectable mixed grill, the half of a blackberry and apple tart smothered in Devonshire cream, and a bottle of the best. By the end of the dinner I had decided to emigrate to England. Some few days later I found myself imbedded in the mud of Salisbury Plain at Bustard Camp, a victim of inclement weather (which penetrated without difficulty the moth-eaten five-ounce canvas of the tent under which I sheltered) and the plaything of loud-voiced and energetic sergeants, who seemed to think that I liked nothing better on a rainy Sunday than to wheel, from the dump to the incinerator a half mile away, the week's collections of garbage. After two weeks of this I decided that I would not live in England.

Believing firmly in the future of aeroplanes and seaplanes in warfare, I made another attempt to transfer to one of the Air Services, the Royal Naval Air Service by preference; for having knocked about a good deal in small boats on the Great Lakes, I thought that the navigation and seamanship I had picked up might prove useful in seaplane work.

On a personal application to the Admiralty I was informed that Colonials were not required, as they made indifferent officers, that the service had all the fliers they would ever need, and, besides all this, that I was too old. And then it was suggested that I should sign on as a mechanic. I went to Farnborough, the headquarters of the Royal Flying Corps, and saw Sir Hugh Trenchard, then I believe a major, and was informed that I could be put on the waiting list, but found I would have to wait six months before seeing an aeroplane, owing to the wicked shortage of machines.

Being full of enthusiasm and impatience, and thinking that the war would be sharp and quick arid soon decided one way or the other, I had another try at the Admiralty. But this time, on the advice of a friend who had lived some time in England, I attacked them in a different way. At my first interview I had appeared with my flying credentials and in the uniform of a private a uniform, as being the King's, of which I was tremendously proud, although the tunic was about two sizes too small for me and the breeches four sizes too large. The second time I wore a suit of civilians cut by a good tailor and carried letters of introduction from sundry important people. I was this time offered a commission as a machinegun Sub-Lieutenant, R.N.V.R., in the armoured cars attached to the Royal Naval Air Service, and believing that this was a step in the right direction, and fully determined to fly at the first opportunity, I was duly gazetted in December 1914.

I was told to report to H.M.S. *Excellent* for training. At the railway station at Portsmouth I asked a taxi-cab driver if he knew where H.M.S. *Excellent* was lying, and he replied that he did, and that he would drive me right on board. I thought that she must be a very big ship, but said nothing. Finally I found myself being driven over a bridge, and was informed a moment later that I was on board H.M.S. *Excellent*, or, in other words, at Whale Island. This training centre is the forcing-house of naval discipline, and everything is done at the double an exceedingly fast double when the eye of the First Lieutenant falls upon an instructor. She is a curious ship. The Captain, when he comes on board by launch from the mainland, is driven up from the landing stage to his office in a little green railway carriage drawn by a little green engine.

For some time I trained in England, and finally sailed for the Dardanelles in March 1915. After forty days in Gallipoli in command of a travelling circus of machineguns and machineguns were worth more than gold and precious stones in the first days on the Peninsula, being attached in turn to the Australians in Shrapnel Valley, sundry units at Cape Helles, and finally to the 29th Division in Gully Ravine, where I worked with the 13th Sikhs until they were practically wiped out on June 4 I again found myself in England in July 1915, my arm in a sling and feeling very thin as the result of sand colic, a horrid complaint which seized me the moment I set foot on Turkish soil at Gaba Tepe.

Following a holiday at Sunning-on-Thames, a two-week caravan trip through the New Forrest behind an old horse named Ben a horse with whiskers on its ankles and a three-knot gait and sundry visits to the Admiralty, I was transferred from Lieutenant R.N.V.R. to Acting Flight Lieutenant R.N.A.S. and posted to Hendon Air Station. Here I acted as First Lieutenant to Flight Commander Busteed until July 1916, having a good rest in order to get fit again, with only a few jobs to do, such as digging drains, building roads, altering machines, lecturing to the school on machineguns and bombs, building huts for the men out of packing-cases, doing acceptance and test flights when I had regained some of my energy, and in my spare time learning what I could of the theory and practice of flight from my commanding officer, who very kindly took no end of trouble in assisting me. Then I was given the command when he left for Eastchurch.

Our Mess was livened up about this time by the frequent visits of a senior officer who, arriving about dinner-time, would discuss flying far into the night, turn out at daybreak to fly any machine available no matter what the weather was like, and then, after breakfast, hasten off to the Admiralty. It was a tremendous relief to meet a senior officer who was keen to know everything about flying at first hand, who could deal on paper with flying problems of which he had practical experience, and took the trouble to understand the point of view of the pilots.

Once when a very senior officer, in a very bad temper, was inspecting the station, he was taken into the first shed. "Quiet, very quiet," he said. "You don't seem to be doing much work for the number of men you have got." A trusty Sub. was despatched to the second shed with instructions to have the party of tin-smiths in the annex hammer like mad on a row of empty tanks. When the inspection party entered this shed the senior officer said, shouting to make himself heard above the noise "Better; much better."

During the fall of 1916 many rumours were about concerning the developments of flying-boats at Felixstowe Air Station, along with a few facts from Lieutenant Partridge, R.N.V.R., who had been ground officer at Hendon, until after taking a course in a gunnery school he went to Felixstowe as armament officer. Also the work at Hendon was petering out, the soldiers of the R.F.C. had cast a monocled and covetous eye on the aerodrome, the submarine situation was becoming acute, and the doctor had forbidden me to fly at any altitude. I therefore put in to be transferred to a seaplane station, and was posted in March 1917 to Felixstowe.

Felixstowe town in ordinary times is a summer resort, but owing to the threat of air raids it was practically forsaken by its usual floating population and was heavily garrisoned by the military, the water front being protected by barbed wire and innumerable trenches. The people of the town in times of peace lived on the summer visitors; during the war they lived on the soldiers and airmen.

THREE

When I first rolled up to Felixstowe Air Station I was tremendously impressed by its size. It was enclosed on the three land sides by a high iron fence. As I passed the sentry-box and entered by the main gate, the guardhouse occupied by the ancient marines was on my right, flanked by the kennel of Joe, a ferocious watchdog who had a strong antipathy to anybody in civilian attire. Beside guarding the gate, Joe provided a steady income to the marines, for his puppies fetched good prices. On my left were the ship's office and garage. I entered the former and reported my arrival to the First Lieutenant.

The First Lieutenant of the station was Lieut.-Commander 0. H. K. Macguire, R.N., known as James the One or Number One, who understood discipline, and reigned over an exceedingly fine mess. He ran the station under naval routine, the time being tapped off on a bell, the ship's company being divided into watches, anybody leaving the station "going ashore," and the men for leave, when marching out of the gate, were the "liberty boat." The Navy people, of course, said that the R.N.A.S. was not run on Navy lines, but it was run as close to them as everybody knew how, and as the exigencies of the new weapon permitted. The naval routine and discipline fitted the work of a seaplane station admirably, for the work approximated to that of a ship, where drill is of secondary importance, and speed, skill, and accuracy in carrying out a job of work is of the first importance.

As James the One had a shrewd tongue he was rather feared by the junior officers, especially the Canadians, who hated with a profound hatred the ever-recurring twenty-four-hour job of Duty Officer, during which they could get no sleep in the long watches of the night owing to the continuous ringing of the tel-

Sheds and slipways at Felixstowe

ephone bell. But he instilled discipline into their unruly hearts, which assisted them to carry out their work when subsequently elevated in rank.

He had taken over the station at a time when, owing to rapid growth, the new men were not being digested, and discipline was rather ragged at the edges; but by this time he had the men well in hand. And woe betide the defaulter, standing to attention outside the ship's office in full view of Number One as he sat in an easy-chair on the veranda of the mess, if the unfortunate so much as moved a little finger. The tiger roar which greeted such a disobedience to the order not to move, made every man with a guilty conscience on the station tremble.

On the other hand, he would brook no interference with the rights and privileges of the men, and looked after their interests as regards pay and promotion. Divisions, when the whole ship's company were mustered on the quarter-deck in the morning and at noon, was a marvel of smartness, especially when it is remembered that the men were "tradesmen." The effect was heightened by the attendance of the pipe band, of which Number One was rightly proud.

Leaving the office of the First Lieutenant I stepped out on the quarterdeck. On the mast, on the far side of this gravelled expanse, rippling and snapping in the breeze, flew the white ensign.

Crossing the quarterdeck and steering close to the bright and shining ship's bell, which I passed on my left, I found a path leading to the harbour. The left side of the path was the starting-point of an interminable row of huts for the men. Carrying on, after stumbling over a railway siding, and passing between two of the huge seaplane sheds, of which there were three sheds 300 feet long by 200 feet wide I eventually arrived at the concrete area on the water front.

Before each of the big sheds was a slipway. These were wide wooden gangways running out from the concrete into the harbour and sloping down into the water, and were used for launching the flying-boats.

Here I could look across the harbour and see Harwich and Shotley, the tangle of light cruisers and destroyers lying at anchor in the river, and the outlines of the floating dock in which destroyers, battered by the seas or damaged in contact with the enemy, were lifted out of the water and their hurts attended to. As I stood sniffing in the harbour smells, one of our E-class submarines came slinking in between the guard-ships at the boom, fresh from patrol in the Bight, and wearing that sinister air of stealth and secrecy which marks even the friendliest of submarines.

Walking down the concrete to my left I finally came to the pre-war buildings of the Old Station. These buildings were used by Commander Porte for his experimental work. In the early part of 1914 Commander Porte was in America, at the Curtiss Company works at Hammondsport, where he supervised the designing and testing of the first American type of flying-boat. This boat was constructed with the intention, if it was satisfactory, of attempting to fly the Atlantic. It was a very big machine for that time, although to a modern pilot, familiar with the luxuriously fitted up six-ton boats with two Rolls-Royce engines giving a total of 720 horsepower, she would seem a funny old, cranky, under-engined tub.

On the afternoon of the day war was declared Commander Porte sailed for England, and a little later took over Felixstowe. Sundry copies of the original boat arrived from the United States in 1915. These were comic machines, weighing well under two tons; with two comic engines giving, when they functioned, 180 horsepower; and comic control, being nose heavy with engines on and tail heavy in a glide. And the stout lads who tried impossible feats in them had usually to be towed back by annoyed destroyers.

As the Navy people could not understand anything being made which could not be dropped with safety from a hundred feet, or seaworthy enough to ride out a gale, or as reliable as the coming of the Day of Judgment for the Hun, much criticism and chaff, some good-natured but some not, were worked off by the sailors during this period on both boats and pilots. But improvements went steadily on.

In the fall of 1916 improved and very much bigger flying-boats, built in the United States to specifications supplied by Commander Porte, began to arrive.

By this time Commander Porte had got out several experimental flying-boats. He carried out his plans with a scratch collection of draughtsmen, few with any real knowledge of engineering; with boat-builders and carpenters he had trained himself; and he only obtained the necessary materials by masterly wangling. He frequently started a new boat and then asked the authorities for the grudged permission. But in all things connected with the building of flying-boats his insight amounted to genius, and the different types of boats kept getting themselves born. His latest boat, known unofficially as the Porte Super Baby, or officially as the Felixstowe Fury, a huge triplane with a wing span of 127 feet, a total lifting surface of 3100 square feet, a bottom of three layers of cedar and mahogany half an inch thick, and five engines giving 1800 horsepower, I flew successfully it weighed a total of fifteen tons. On this test I carried twenty-four passengers, seven hours' fuel, and five thousand pounds of sand as a make-weight. Some idea of its huge size can be had when it is realised that its tail unit alone is as large as a modern single-seater scout.

At Hendon I had assisted in dragging the first twin-engined Handley-Page, at midnight and with the greatest secrecy, through the streets leading from the works at Cricklewood to the aerodrome. The procession was headed by an army of men removing obstructing lamp-posts and cutting off overhanging branches, followed by a motor-lorry with two acetylene flares, and then sixty men hauling the machine along by ropes. At the time I thought she was a very big machine. But in the sheds at Felixstowe I found boats of equal size and horsepower and greater speed, and boats that were even larger.

There was the boat called the *Porte Baby*, a bigger machine than any built and flown in this country until 1918, and this boat was produced in 1915 and flown in 1916. Although it did little useful active service work, it set other designers to thinking, and was the father and mother of all big British aeroplanes and seaplanes. When fully loaded it weighed about eight and a half tons, but no scales big enough to weigh it were obtainable in the service.

It was so large that a Bristol Bullet land scout was fitted on the top plane, which, while the boat was in the air, was successfully launched and flown back to an aerodrome by Flight Lieutenant Day, of the seaplane carrier *Vindex*. This gallant officer unfortunately was killed later in France.

Well on in 1917 sundry young pilots took the *Porte Baby* out for a joyride, and presently found themselves off the Belgian coast being attacked by a Hun land-machine and two fighter seaplanes. Two out of the three engines were shot about and the big boat had to come down on the water. The Huns circled around firing at it until their ammunition was exhausted, and then returned joyously to Zeebrugge to report the total destruction of a giant flying-boat.

But while the tracer bullets were playing about, the crew were lying down in the bottom of the boat watching the splinters fly. When the Huns departed the crew repaired the engines, started them up, and all night long taxied on the water across the North Sea. The much-chastened pilots beached the boat, in the small hours of the morning, on the coast of England, near Orford Ness. A sentry, believing, as he explained later, that at last an invasion of England by Zeppelin was being attempted, fired on them, but was eventually pacified. The crew arrived at the station very tired, very black, one of their number with a bullet hole in him, but cheerful.

When the *Porte Baby* was finally dismantled, her hull was placed in the grounds of a woman's hostel, a door was cut in the side, electric light laid on, and four Wren motor-drivers found sufficient room inside to sling their hammocks, stow clothing, and room even for mirrors and powder puffs.

After sculling about in the sheds for some time, I finally climbed to the lookout on top of Number One Shed.

Here I surveyed for the first time the mottled, misty, treacherous North Sea. In a south-easterly direction and some ninety miles away was the Belgian coast, with the German submarine and seaplane bases at Zeebrugge and Ostend. Some hundred and eighty miles away, in a north-easterly direction, was Terschelling Island, and just around the corner of this island was the Bight of Heligoland. On a shoal, half-way on a line between Felixstowe and the Hook of Holland, fifty-two sea miles from either place and the same distance from Zeebrugge, was the red rusty North Hinder light-vessel belonging to the Dutch, with a large lantern on its one stout steel mast, and its name painted in huge white letters along its sides. This light-vessel was to play a large part in the bombing of submarines.

FOUR

After some days at Felixstowe, feeling rather like a lost dog, as no work had been given me to do, and always expecting some demonstration to be made against the German submarines, I was much disappointed to find that nothing seemed to be done.

Indeed, I got exceedingly mouldy, so mouldy that I broke out in verses for *The Wing*, the station magazine. They were a lament for the old land hack I had left behind at Hendon a scandalous biplane, which had been rebuilt so often that nobody could tell the breed. Her fabric was so ancient that on the last time I had flown her the covering on the top side of the centre section had blown off. The verses ran:

To My Old Bus

To Number One she's ullage and he's ordered her deletion,
For the grease and dirt are ingrained, and she isn't smart as paint,
And the flat-foot X-Y-Chaser helped by calling her a horror
Although she's sweet to handle, which some experts' buses ain't.

I've tumbled split-all endwise in her from a bank of vapour,
And surprised a little rainbow lying sleeping in a cloud;
I did my first loop in her, and I've crashed her and rebuilt her,
And robbed her spares from other planes, which strictly ain't allowed.

At evening, just at sunset, I have climbed into her cockpit,
And gone roaring up an air lane till I've caught the sun again,
And feeling most important at my private view of glory,
Have watched him set splendacious with his pink and golden train.

Her crash form's all in order, and they'll strip, saw, break, and burn her,
And I'm sorry more than I can say to know she has to go;
For blue, depressed, fed-up, or sore, I'd but to climb aboard her
To leave my pack of mouldy troubles far away below.

The patrol work of the station was rather at a low ebb at this time through various causes. With the machines available much good work had been done in the previous years, but the first five big twin engine-boats to be erected and tested, together with many good pilots and engineers, had just boomed off for the Scilly Islands, leaving a rather large hole in the station resources. Weather conditions also were not very good. There was no organisation in existence for carrying out intensive anti-submarine patrol, and there appeared to be no signs of that passionate energy by which alone, in all branches of anti-submarine work, the knavish tricks of the U-boat were frustrated.

A great deal of the energy of the station was taken up in experimental work and the erection of flying-boats, of which forty in all were assembled, fitted out, and tested during the year.

The engines of the only two boats available for patrol, Nos. 8661 and 8663, were run and tested every morning before daybreak, but after volunteering many times to get up and run the engines, I found that the boats never went out. There was a feeling among the majority of the pilots at this time that there was little use in patrols from Felixstowe, as from the beginning of the war only two enemy submarines had been sighted by pilots on patrol from the station. This lack of success was not due to patrols not having been done, although intensive work had never been carried out owing to the lack of suitable machines, but was due to the few submarines that had been navigating about.

But now the enemy submarines were freely and copiously navigating the narrow seas, and the Zeppelins were nonchalantly parading in daylight outside the Bight of Heligoland.

Commander Porte, owing to various causes, was absent from Felixstowe for long periods throughout this year, although fortunately his advice and experience were available for operations. Number One, who was in charge in the absence of Commander Porte, was not a flying officer, but he appreciated the situation, saw the Senior Naval Officer, Harwich, under whose command the operations came, and obtained a tremendous concession from him. This was, that Felixstowe was given permission to carry out anti-submarine patrol on its own, providing that he approved of the general scheme and was kept informed of the movements of machines.

Our S.N.O. was unlike some other Senior Naval Officers under whose command for operations there were float seaplanes and boats. For some of them did not know the technical and weather limitations, and therefore frequently ordered impossibilities, and when failure resulted, damned the machines and personnel of the Royal Naval Air Service; on the other hand they would not allow possible operations to be carried out which they had not originated themselves.

In sketching out the campaign from Felixstowe against the U-boats, it was decided that the only sure method of protecting shipping was to damage or destroy submarines, and that all other methods were merely palliative. It was considered that ships proceeding in the shipping lane, which was close to the coast of England and protected by shallow minefields and surface patrol craft, were well looked after, and that enemy submarines, if operating in these busy waters, would be so on the alert and keep such a good lookout that the flying-boats would not be given a chance; for submarines cannot be seen from the air when once below the surface of the North Sea. It was therefore decided to expend all available flying time where submarines were to be found on the surface, and that the efficiency of the patrols would not be decided by the number of flying hours put in, but by the number of submarines sighted and bombed.

The Hun submarines streaming down through the southern portion of the North Sea were of the U-B, U-C, and U types

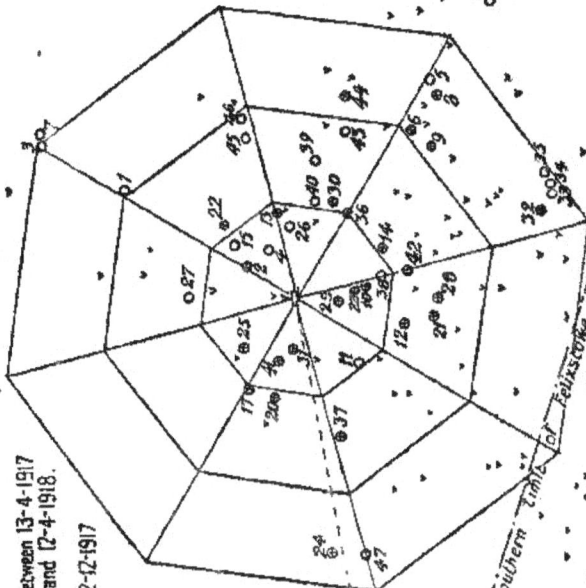

HOOK OF
HOLLAND

N

Zeebrugge

STRAIT OF DOVER

FELIXSTOWE PATROL AREA WITH SPIDER WEB PATROL

RIVER THAMES

Ipswich
Felixstowe
Harwich

Southern Trials
Felixstowe Area

2450

the smallest 90 feet in length and the largest 225 feet long. They were mine-layers and commerce destroyers, and their commanders travelled on the surface through the Felixstowe area, because the distance they could go under water was only about seventy-five miles, and they could only run submerged at eight knots for two hours before exhausting their electric batteries. And low speeds say of two knots, which the submarine could keep up for forty-eight hours when submerged were of no value to an impatient Fritz anxious to get to his hunting-ground. And this was important, as the hundred-mile stretch of water between England and Holland is very shallow, and consequently muddy, and presents a brown and dirty green mottled surface opaque to the eye of the observer in the air.

The exact position of the German submarines was obtained from time to time; for when their commanders reported to Germany by wireless which they usually did when homeward bound after making up through the Straits of Dover safely, although sometimes they reported when southbound the signal betrayed their position. The wireless messages were picked up by two direction-finding wireless stations in England, each station obtaining a bearing of the U-boat that was sending. When the two bearings obtained in this way were plotted out on the chart they crossed, and where they crossed there the U-boat had been. This was known as a wireless fix.

The wireless fixes of the submarines showed that they were passing in the vicinity of the North Hinder light-vessel; so a method of carrying out the search was devised, and this was called the Spider Web.

This tremendous spider web was sixty miles in diameter. It allowed for the searching of four thousand square miles of sea, and was right across the path of the submarines. A submarine ten miles outside of it was in danger of being spotted, so at cruising speed it took ten hours for a U-boat to cross it. Under ordinary conditions a boat could search two sectors that is, a quarter of the whole web in five hours or less. The tables were turned on Fritz the hunter; for here he was the hunted, the quarry, the fly that had to pass through some part of the web. The flying-boat was the spider.

The Spider Web Patrol was based on the North Hinder light-vessel, which was used as a centre point, and allowed for a thorough searching of the sea in a forty-mile radius. It was an octagonal figure with eight radial arms thirty sea-miles in length, and with three sets of circumferential lines joining the arms ten, twenty, and thirty miles out from the centre. Eight sectors were thus provided for patrol, and all kinds of combinations could be worked out. As the circumferential lines were ten miles apart, each section of a sector was searched twice on any patrol when there was good visibility.

A chart was kept showing the positions, dates, and times of day that submarines were fixed by wireless, and it was from this chart that the sectors which would pay for searching were determined.

The pilots were to boom out from Felixstowe to the North Hinder, a distance of fifty-two sea-miles, fly out a radial arm as instructed, and then proceed along the patrol lines in the sectors to be searched, sweeping from the outside to the centre, returning to the North Hinder and so to the base.

Navigation over the sea, where one square mile of water looks exactly like every other square mile, is more difficult than finding the way over land. The only fixed objects by which a pilot can check his calculated position are light-vessels and buoys, but in wartime these are shifted about, and there are large areas without any such marks.

The difficulty of navigation is due to the fact that unless there is absolutely no wind, the compass, after the corrections for variation and deviation are made, only shows the direction in which the head of the flying-boat is pointing and not the direction in which it is travelling, and the air-speed indicator only gives the speed of the machine in relation to the air.

For an aircraft is completely immersed in the air, so that besides its movement in relation to the air caused by its own mechanism, it moves with the air over the surface of the earth, the speed and path of the machine being the result of the two movements.

If the pilot of a flying-boat had to go to a lightship sixty miles due east from his station when a twenty-knot wind was blowing from the north, and he flew at sixty knots due east by his compass, at the end of an hour he would not fetch up at his object, but twenty miles to the south of it. If, instead of flying on 90 degrees, which is east, he flew on 71 degrees on his compass, he would fetch up at the lightship in sixty-three minutes, having travelled due east over the surface of the sea. To a man in a ship he would appear to be flying sideways.

Similarly, if a pilot flew into a sixty-knot wind with his air-speed indicator showing sixty knots, he would not be moving over the surface of the sea, and to the man in the ship he would appear to be standing still.

The Chaplain of the station, the Rev. W. G. Litchfield, produced for us a simple table with which the pilot, knowing approximately the force and direction of the wind, could quickly work out the compass correction for drift and the time correction for the air-speed indicator.

The patrols were to be carried out at the height of a thousand feet, because at this height silhouettes of the submarines and surface craft could best be seen, the run of the wind on the water could be spotted and its direction and force determined, and it was easy to drop down to eight hundred or six hundred feet to bomb a Fritz.

Being now ready to start, and being given the sounding title of Commanding Officer War Flight, I had No. 2 shed, the two boats 8661 and 8663, and an insufficient number of men turned over to me.

There was no intelligence hut, no flying office, no telephone in the shed, no pigeons; and Billiken Hobbs, who was the only pilot at this time turned over to the flight, had never seen an enemy submarine. And I was in like case myself; besides which, I had never flown one of the big twin-engined boats.

On the afternoon of April 12 all arrangements had been made.

CHAPTER 2

Like a Fairy Tale

ONE

The first eighteen days of the life of the War Flight was like a fairy tale, for the pilots, booming out on the Spider Web in the wet triangle formed by the Shipwash light-vessel, the Haaks lightship, and the Schouen Bank light-buoy, sighted eight enemy submarines and bombed three, one of the patrols ran into four Hun destroyers and was heavily shelled, and one boat was lost at sea, although all members of the crew were saved.

On the morning of April 13 we carried out the first patrol of the series, patrols which were to make the southern portion of the North Sea unhealthy for Fritz to travel through on his unlawful occasions.

I had hot-stuffed a big brass ship's bell from the Old Station, put up a neat white gibbet to carry it in No. 2 shed, polished it, hung it up, and fitted to its clapper a neatly grafted bell lanyard finished off with a Turk's-head knot. At ten o'clock on this day, a day with an overcast sky and a twenty-knot westerly wind blowing, I sounded off five sharp taps on the bell, the signal for patrol. The chiefs of the engineer, carpenter, and working parties reported for instructions, and the working party fell in ready to move machines.

Trim, clean, grey, and rigged true, and just tipping the scales at four and a half tons, No. 8661 stood on her wheeled land trolley just inside the shed. She was a fine machine, measuring ninety-six feet from wing tip to wing tip, and had such a long and honourable life, doing three hundred hours of patrol work, and three hundred and sixty-eight hours flying in all, that she was affectionately known to all the pilots as *Old '61*. Her 42-foot wooden hull, covered with canvas above the water-line, was flat-bottomed and had a hydroplane step, which lifted her on top of the water when she was getting off, and so enabled her to obtain a speed at which the wings had sufficient lift to pick her up into the air.

She carried six and a half hours' fuel at a cruising speed of sixty knots, her top speed being eighty. A knot is a speed of one nautical mile an hour, and a nautical mile is 800 feet longer than a statute or land mile, so that full out she could do ninety-two land miles an hour.

The working party of twenty men gathered around *Old '61* and rolled her out of the shed to the concrete area. Here they chocked her up under the bow and tail with trestles in order to prevent her standing on her nose when the engines were tested. Two engineers climbed up to each engine and started them. After they had been run slowly for about fifteen minutes in order to warm up the oil, they were opened out until they were giving their full revolutions, the tremendous power shaking the whole structure of the boat.

In the meantime the armourers' party had fitted on the four Lewis machineguns and had tucked up into place under the wing roots, two on each side of the hull, the four one hundred pound bombs. The bombs were fitted with a delay action fuse which detonated them about two seconds after they hit the water or a submarine. If they hit the water they would detonate when from sixty to eighty feet below the surface.

Bombs detonated near a submarine might merely shake her,

fuse cut-outs and extinguish electric lights, which was very bad for the moral of the Hun crew and lowered their efficiency. Or they might cause a leak, say by buckling a hatch, which the pumps could not keep under; or puncture the external oil-tanks, which would cause a large loss of oil fuel; or the periscope bases might be shaken or damaged; or the hydroplanes might be forced hard up or hard down, making them difficult to work and causing the boat to get out of control. All of which things would make the commander of the submarine return to port and so save merchant shipping. Or such serious damage might be caused that the submarine would immediately sink. Direct hits usually destroyed a submarine. In the early part of the war a U-boat was sunk by the direct hit of a sixteen-pound bomb.

When the boat was ready we climbed on board. Billiken Hobbs was the First Pilot, I was the Second Pilot, and there were the wireless operator and the engineer.

Master of seven hundred roaring horsepower, responsible for all things connected with the operation of the boat, and having to make instant and correct decisions as to the nationality of submarines seen at strange angles and oddly foreshortened, the first pilot of a flying boat had to be a very fine fellow indeed. He was the captain, and took the boat off the harbour and brought her in again, flew her on the hunting-ground and in an air fight, and saw that the remainder of the crew knew and did their duty.

From the repairing of the boats and the handling of them on shore, to the dropping of a bomb on a submarine, it was not a sport but a business, a business that had to be learned, and the making of a good first pilot was a longer task than the making of a land machine pilot. Good first pilots were few, and when found were usually worked until they cracked under the strain. For the stress due to steering careful compass courses for hours is considerable, the effort of keeping a constant and efficient lookout is very tiring, and the early boats were either tail heavy or nose heavy, which threw a strain on the heart of the pilot. Canadians seemed to be best fitted for flying-boat work, and probably as high a proportion as three-fourths of the good boat pilots came from that dominion.

Billiken took his seat in a little padded armchair on the right-hand side of the control cockpit, a cockpit which ran across the full width of the boat some distance back from the nose. He was covered in by a transparent wheel-house so that he did not have to wear goggles, an important point in submarine hunting, as goggles interfere with efficient observation.

Before him on the instrument board was the compass, the air-speed indicator, the altimeter which showed the height above the sea, a bubble cross level which indicated if the boat was correctly balanced laterally, the inclinometer which gave the fore-and-aft angle at which the boat was flying, the oil-pressure gauges, and the engine revolution counters. Close to his hand were the engine switches and the throttle control levers. Immediately in front of him was an eighteen-inch wheel, like the wheel of a motor-car, but carried vertically upright on a wooden yoke, with which he controlled the boat when in the air. He worked the steering rudder with his feet.

As Second Pilot I stood beside Billiken. If a submarine was sighted I ducked forward into the cockpit in the very nose of the boat, where I had my machinegun, bomb sight, and the levers which released the bombs. In a little handbook, got out by a very wily first pilot for the benefit of second pilots, a few of the hints as to their duties are as follows:

"Commence your watch-keeping at once and report to your first pilot buoys, lightships, wrecks, or other objects which may enable him to establish his position. Don't take it for granted that he has seen anything that you have seen until you have pointed it out.

"Observe above, below, around, in front, and behind.

"You must be prepared to give your position to your first pilot or wireless operator without hesitation at any moment throughout the patrol. Make a small pencil circle on your track on the chart every fifteen miles or so and at every alteration in course, writing the time against this mark.

"When dropping bombs remember they will only function if fused.

"If a crash is inevitable, and you can save anything, four things should take precedence pigeons, emergency rations, Very's lights, and the Red Cross outfit.

"Learn how to tie a bowline. This is the simplest, quickest, and most reliable knot for making fast your machine to a tow-line. Learn other knots too.

"Study the methods of handling machines on the slipway, both going out and coming in. You may be in charge of this operation some day, and the responsibility will be yours.

"In short, make this the *moral*:

"Know the boat and all that therein and thereon is, thorough-ly, and its capabilities and efficiencies, if you wish to become not only a good pilot, but capable of command. This information is acquired from time spent in the sheds and not from time spent reclining on wardroom settees."

The wireless operator had climbed into his place and sat fac-ing forward on the right-hand side of the boat immediately behind Billiken. He had his wireless cabinet, containing his in-struments, before him, and could send and receive for a distance of from eighty to a hundred miles. He coded and decoded all signals. The code-book had weighted covers, so that if the boat were captured by the enemy it would sink immediately when thrown overboard. He had an Aldis signalling-lamp for commu-nicating with ships and other flying-boats. He also looked after the Red Cross box, which contained a tourniquet, first-aid kit, the sandwiches for immediate needs, the emergency rations for five days, and the carrier-pigeons.

The engineer was in his cockpit in the middle of the boat, surrounded by the petrol-tanks, a maze of piping, and innumer-able gadgets. His duties were to keep an eye on the engines, see that the water in the radiators did not boil, and take care of the petrol system.

Two wind-driven pumps forced the petrol up from the main tanks to a small tank in the top plane. The engines were fed from the top tank by gravity, and the surplus petrol pumped up ran back to the main tanks. The engineer regulated the flow so that the petrol was drawn from and overflowed back into the main tanks in such a way that the fore-and-aft balance of the boat was maintained. If anything went wrong with an engine he had to climb out on the wing and, if possible, make a repair.

Once a flying-boat attacked a submarine from a low altitude, and was met by machinegun fire. A bullet drilled a hole in a radiator, and the water began to run out. Also the first two bombs dropped missed the submarine. The engineer quickly climbed out on the wing and put a plug in the hole, and held it there, while the pilot took the boat over the submarine again, and destroyed it with the second two bombs. The engineer held the plug in place until the boat landed in the home harbour.

All four members of the crew were now in their places. The working party attached a stout line to the rear of the trolley, knocked away the chocks, and rolled the boat out on the slipway to where it began to slope down into the water. Here six waders, in waterproof breeches coming up to their armpits, and weighted boots to give them a secure foothold when the tide was running, took charge, and steered the boat down into the water, the working party easing her down by tailing on the line.

A wader has not got a soft job. At some stations where there is a strong tide running waders have been washed off the slipways and drowned.

As the flying-boat entered the water the trolley, being heavy, remained on the slipway, and the boat floated off. The thrust of the engines urged her forward, and she taxied clear. Hobbs taxied out into the harbour, turned up into the wind, and opened the engines full out.

Driven by seven hundred tearing horsepower, the boat ran along the water with ever-increasing speed, a big white wave bursting into spray beneath her bow. As the speed increased, the boat was lifted on top of the water by her hydroplane step until she was skimming lightly over the surface. The air speed-indicator was registering thirty-five knots. Then Hobbs pulled back the control wheel, and the boat leaped into the air, the air speed jumping to sixty knots. Climbing in a straight line until he was at a thousand feet, he turned the bow of the boat out to sea.

As much doubt had been expressed about the practicability of flying the Spider Web Patrol, owing to the great number of changes in course and the absence of lightships and buoys, it was decided to do the patrol without any windage allowance. We made the North Hinder light-vessel dead on, and then started on the Web. Finally, as the wind was westerly, we fetched up on the Dutch coast, the low white sand-hills of which I now saw for the first time. Coming back against a head-wind, it took so long that I thought at first that somebody had moved England, and being very tired, I lay down in the bottom of the boat and had a sleep.

I was awakened when we were in sight of the Shipwash light-vessel a vessel with a single black ball as a day mark carried at the mast head. She was eighteen sea miles from Felixstowe, four miles off the route from the North Hinder, and many a pilot, bathed in perspiration with the stress of handling his boat in bad weather, or coming in out of the North Sea against a head wind with nearly empty tanks, has been cheered by the sight of the short dumpy boat champing at its anchor chains.

We saw no submarines on this patrol, but it proved that there was no difficulty in flying the Spider Web under ordinary conditions.

Two

After the first patrol had been carried out four more pilots volunteered for the War Flight, and two patrols were carried out on April 15th. It was on the fourth patrol, on the 16th, that Billiken Hobbs, booming along in the Web at the thousand foot level in *Old '61*, sighted the first enemy submarine.

The commander of this U-boat was gaily navigating along on the surface, fully blown, at a position twenty miles north-east of the North Hinder. He was feeling quite at ease, for the visibility was good and the surface of the sea was clear; he was too far out to be molested by trawlers, and if destroyers hove in sight he could dive to a depth of 45 feet in ninety seconds. The hull of his boat was painted grey and the decks black, making it very difficult to see.

Had he been expecting trouble he would have been running awash that is, with the conning-tower alone showing above water, and with one electric motor and one Diesel-engine going. He could then have done a "crash" dive in about thirty seconds, going under with hydroplanes hard down, full weigh on, and taking in water ballast.

But he did not know about the flying-boats or the Spider Web.

He was standing in the conning-tower beside the lookout man. He may have been thinking of his sweetheart at home, or the faces of the men and women he had drowned, but he certainly was not keeping a good lookout. For he suddenly saw a black shape like a great crow in the distance, and immediately afterwards a long grey boat, fitted with wings, passed immediately over him.

When the crew of the flying-boat first sighted the submarine the second pilot fired two recognition signals, and as no answer was made Billiken decided it was a Fritz. He took the flying-boat across it at the height of eight hundred feet, but the second pilot in the front cockpit, not having been trained in bomb dropping, failed to release the bombs. Swinging the boat round in a split-all bank he again passed over, but again the second pilot failed to pull the release levers, pulling instead at the bowden wires, which came away from their fastenings.

Recovering from his astonishment, the Commander of the submarine realised that the flying-boat was there with no very friendly intentions, and tapped the lookout man beside him on the shoulder, at which signal the latter dropped through the hatchway in the conning-tower down into the boat. The Commander then pressed a button which rang the alarm bells below, and the men at the hydroplane wheels and ballast cocks caused the boat to dive.

5-TON FLYING-BOAT

As she began to submerge he shut down the hatch of the conning-tower and the submarine slowly vanished from the sight of the infuriated Billiken.

The second pilot, poor lad, was killed in a small float seaplane a short time afterwards, by ramming a flying-boat with which he was practising fighting, and so had no second chance at a submarine.

When the submarine was sighted the wireless operator had got off a quick signal to the station, so when the first faint intermittent roar of the twin engines of *Old '61* could be heard, and she was seen as a small black speck over the wreck of the Dutch steamer *Juliana*, mined early in the war, the whole ship's company seemed to have found work to do on the slipways and concrete area. Ten men were preventing each other from coiling down a hawser, twenty men were noisily rolling empty petrol barrels about, and innumerable men were shifting trolleys or merely standing still and trying to look busy.

The sheds and the workshops were deserted.

As Billiken boomed in over the harbour and shut off his engines to glide down, somebody on the slipway cried: "He's dropped his bombs." And everybody cheered. And then a man with binoculars shouted: "He hasn't dropped them," and thrust the glasses into the hand of the man next to him so that he could verify it.

When the motor-boat had taken *Old '61* in tow and tied her up to a buoy, the crew were brought ashore. The two pilots were almost mobbed by the officers, and the wireless operator and engineer were surrounded by great groups of men to whom they told the tale. It was not very long, however, before a flying-boat could come into the harbour after bombing a submarine without anybody looking up from his work.

There was considerable excitement in the mess that night. Great enthusiasm had seized everybody. They realised that there were submarines outside and that they could be seen and bombed, and there was a tremendous surge of pilots asking to join the War Flight. In all, another eight pilots were taken on.

And then the gilt was put on the gingerbread, for on the eighth patrol Monk Aplin presented a Fritz with four one hundred pound bombs. Fritz saw the flying-boat coming and ducked, but the swirl where he had gone down was still showing on the surface when the four heavy underwater explosions occurred right across his probable path.

The success of the War Flight was now assured.

Eager young pilots waited on the padre to gather wisdom concerning aerial navigation, and went about muttering strange things about "variation, deviation, triangle of forces, and courses made good." Uncle Partridge, the armament officer, was running a continuous performance for their benefit entitled: "Bomb the Boche Boys, or Frightfulness for Fritz." Spring-heel Jack Lyons, the wireless merchant, whose shore aerial was a makeshift affair attached to a stick on top of a shed, panicked for a proper wireless outfit. And C.G. Carlisle, the Old Man of the Sea, approving of the activity, put some ginger into the working party and the crews of the motor-boats.

The Old Man of the Sea, or Jumbo, as he was called, because of his appearance and methods on the football field, was an institution on the station. He was in charge of the working party which did all the pulley-hauley work, and of the piratical crews of the motor-boats who looked after the flying-boats when they were on the water of the harbour. He had all sorts of fascinating model sheerlegs and derricks for training his men, and on occasion headed the salvage crew or the wrecking gang.

He was a merchant service officer who had spent thirteen years at sea, part of the time fetching oil from Patagonia, and it was rumoured that he had also fetched from that salubrious spot his picturesque language. Some weekend trippers to Felixstowe, standing outside the barbed wire enclosing the beach, after watching and hearing, with eyes popping out and ears flapping, the unconscious Jumbo handling a working party bringing in the *Porte Baby*, wrote an anonymous letter to the Commanding Officer complaining of the earache, and adding, "it was Sunday too." This effusion was signed "A Disgusted

Visitor." It was quite evident that the writer had never been with our armies in Flanders.

When the War Flight was first started Jumbo had palmed off on me, being new in the mess, all the halt, lame, and blind for a working party, for he had a habit of secreting away all the best men for nefarious jobs of his own. But after the first submarine was bombed his heart was completely softened, and with a great wrench, and protesting that his own work would never get done, he turned over to me one man who knew his job.

THREE

It was on the eleventh patrol carried out on the 23rd that I bombed my first submarine.

On a pleasant morning, with a clear sky, a slight haze, and a 15-knot wind blowing from the north-east ideal weather conditions for submarine hunting Holmes and myself were shoved down the slipway in *Old '61* and took to the air at six o'clock. Thrusting out into the North Sea on a course for the North Hinder, I steadied at the thousand foot level and throttled back until we were doing an easy sixty knots.

Looking back inside the boat I saw the wireless operator doing a pantomime of unwinding a reel, and I nodded to him, at which he began to let down the aerial through the tube in the bottom of the boat. This was a copper wire three hundred feet long with a weight attached to the end.

If the boat was on the water this trailing aerial could of course not be used, so a telescopic wooden mast was carried. The top of this mast when it was set up was about thirty feet above the surface of the water, and the aerial was led from the bow, tail, and ends of the upper plane to the tip. With this aerial the operator could send and receive for a distance of about thirty miles. Before these masts were carried a boat came down at sea through engine trouble near a lightship. The first pilot made the flying-boat fast to the stern of the light-vessel and the wireless operator led the aerial to its mast. In this way the shore station was called up and a ship was sent out to tow in the disabled boat.

After passing over the well-known buoys at the approaches to the harbour, we crossed a fleet of trawlers in the emergency war channel busily engaged in the pleasing task of sweeping up enemy mines laid the evening before by an optimistic Fritz from Zeebrugge. Fifteen minutes later we had the Shipwash four miles on our port beam, and were over the shipping channel which ran parallel with the coast. Here, as far as the eye could see in either direction, was a thick stream of cargo boats, of all shapes and sizes, ploughing along on their various occasions, a striking example of the might of the British Mercantile Marine.

My ears were now deadened to the noise of the engines, and I would not hear them again unless something went wrong and the note changed. I had got the feel of the controls and was flying automatically, and was unconscious of being in the air. It was merely like rushing over a very calm sea in a fast motor-boat, except for the absence of shocks and the wide horizon.

Leaving the shipping channel behind we pushed on into the open sea. Presently Holmes slapped me on the shoulder and pointed over the starboard bow. Some seven miles away were four white waves rushing across the surface of the water, apparently without any means of propagation. Taking my hands from the control-wheel I made the signal "washout," on recognising the bow-waves of four destroyers in line ahead pushing through the water at top speed, although the low, slim, grey ships were invisible, and of course no Huns would be playing about in such dangerous parts.

The wireless operator came forward for the crew of a flying-boat can move about easily and change places if necessary lifted the flap in the side of my flying-cap, and shouted in my ear "Hun submarine working. Heading towards her." All the four of us were now keeping a keen lookout, my own method being to swing my head from side to side with a slow steady motion, thoroughly searching the half-circle of the horizon, keeping my eyes focussed for a distance of four miles, as this was the average distance for sighting submarines, although they have been sighted from a distance of fifteen miles.

And then I saw a black speck on the water dead ahead. Involuntarily I shoved down the nose of the boat and opened out the engines. And then I saw that it was the North Hinder. As we passed over her the Dutch flag at her stern was politely dipped in salute. Changing course here we boomed off towards the Schouen Bank buoy on the first arm of the Spider Web.

Suddenly, with a nerve shock, a pleasant tingling which cannot be described, I saw a submarine dead ahead, about five miles away, fully blown, and running directly towards us. Slamming on the engines, and pushing the controls forward so as to lose height and gain the maximum speed quickly, I hurled the 4½-ton machine through the air towards the submarine at a mile and a half a minute.

As our own submarines operated in this area I did not know whether it was a Fritz, but fervently hoped it was.

I noticed that it was running at about six knots, in which case it was probably a Hun travelling on one engine and charging the batteries with the dynamo on the other. The submarine statement received from the Naval authorities the evening before had not mentioned one of our own submarines as working in this vicinity, but then submarines were a law unto themselves as regards time and navigation, and had a habit of appearing in the most unexpected places.

With the opening of the engines, the signal for action stations, the engineer thrust himself up in the rear cockpit and seized the stern guns in case hostile seaplanes had been sighted, the wireless operator quickly wound in his trailing aerial to prevent it being carried away if the boat came down near the water, and Holmes, who had seen the submarine, ducked into the front cockpit. He snapped back the lever which removed the safety device from the bombs and set the bomb-sight for height, speed, and wind.

When a bomb is released it travels forward on the same line as the machine, and, at first, at the same speed, but its speed forward gradually diminishes owing to the resistance of the air. At the same time it travels downwards owing to the force of gravity at an ever increasing rate of speed. It thus reaches the surface of the sea just after the machine has passed vertically over the spot. Therefore a bomb is released some time before the machine is vertically over the target, and this time is determined by the speed of the machine over the sea, the height at which it is flying, and the size, shape, and weight of the bomb. All these factors are worked out on the bomb-sight, and the bomb-dropper has only to pull the release-lever when two projections on the sight and the target are in line.

Holmes, in the front cockpit, looking over the sight and with his hand on the release-lever, waited.

The broad white wake behind the submarine began to diminish in length and width. The deck disappeared beneath a tumble of broken water. The conning-tower alone showed. And then the submarine dived.

It had all the air of performing a clever sleight-of-hand trick, and vanished with such lazy insolence that, arriving over the place where it had gone down one minute too late, our hearts were filled with astonishment and anger.

There was nothing to be done. "See you later," we said, and carried on, for we knew that the Spider Web would bring us back again to the same place, and we reasoned that the Commander of the submarine would say, "Here she comes, and there she goes," and would come to the surface shortly. There was no use waiting around the vicinity, for before Fritz came up he would search the air with a "sky-scraping" periscope, a periscope with the lenses so arranged that the whole arc of the heavens could be viewed.

Pushing on we sighted the Schouen Bank buoy in the distance through binoculars, and turned north up the Dutch coast. On the next two legs of the patrol, more or less parallel with the shore, we broke out the package of sandwiches and broached the thermos flask, taking this opportunity of having a drop of early lunch. Then after steering various courses as requisite, we again approached the position where the submarine had been first sighted.

She was sighted again three miles on the port bow, fully blown, her engines stopped, and the crew on deck enjoying a breath of fresh air. But now we were near enough to recognise her as of the U-B class, from the one gun mounted close before the conning-tower, the deck sloping down aft to the stern where it was awash, and the net-cutter mounted above the stem.

As we burst on towards the U-boat full out at a height of six hundred feet we could see puffs of smoke coming from the conning-tower. The crew were firing at us with a pom-pom.

And then I lost sight of the submarine.

But Holmes in the front cockpit, with his view unobstructed by the hull of the boat, could still see the submarine and guided me by hand signal.

Keeping my eyes in the boat, watching the cross level to keep on an even keel, the air-speed indicator to keep to a steady speed, and the eloquent hand for under these circumstances the hand almost seems to talk to make small adjustments in the course, I waited. For, to do good bomb-dropping the boat must pass on a line vertically over the submarine, on an even keel, and at a constant speed.

As the sights came on Holmes pulled the release-lever, which dropped all the bombs in quick succession, threw up his arm to show that he had done so, and then, leaning far over the side, saw the four bombs travelling forward and down-ward and burst on a line diagonally across the submarine.

When the dunt of the first explosion shook the flying-boat I heaved her over on one wing-tip, so that I could look down and back, and saw a line of foam completely across the submarine, so closely had the bombs fallen together. And then, getting into a side slip, I had to attend to my flying duties. The engineer saw the submarine heel over to port and disappear with men still on the conning-tower.

At ten o'clock I landed *Old '61* on the harbour, and not knowing whether the submarine had been sunk or only dam-aged, I immediately sent out another boat. An hour later, piloted by Billiken, I again pushed out on patrol, but returned without having seen any signs of the U-boat, having put in during the day nine hours and fifteen minutes in the air.

FOUR

The quality of the dental platinum, requisitioned from the dentists to make points for the magnetos, brought the first boat down at sea on the eleventh patrol. This platinum, specially prepared for dental work, was not up to the job, and Jimmy Bath and Tiny Galpin had to come to the water forty-five miles out from land. They were found by a destroyer and towed in.

John O. Galpin known as Tiny, because of his comfortable proportions was, as he said himself, followed by a hoodoo. He held at this time the record for the greatest number of engine failures out at sea in float seaplanes, and was quite hardened to spending the night adrift.

At this time, if he got up early in the morning on a fine day to go out on patrol, while he was having breakfast it would rain. If it did not rain, the engines would refuse to start. If the engines started, he would be delayed in getting away by finding there was no petrol in the tanks. If he got away, he would get to the point in his patrol farthest from shore and have engine failure. If he was picked up by a destroyer, there would be a collision and his machine would be sunk. And if none of these things happened to him, and he arrived home safely by air, all the submarines had been navigating in other waters.

He describes the state of affairs in *The Wing* as follows:

Cheerioh!

The Seaplane is my Hoodoo,
I shall not fly another,
It maketh me to come down on rough waters,
It spoileth my reputation.
Though I fly from the harbour
It returneth by towing.
Its Magneto discomforts me.
Its tank runneth over.

49

Its rods and its engines fail me.
Yea, even by mechanics is my name held in laughter.
Though I strive to overcome them
Its weaknesses prevail.
In the hour of my need its engines mock me
And bring me down with great bumpings,
And there is no health in it.
Verily, verily, if I continue to fly these things
I shall end by drowning;
For my friends they desert me
And call me a Jonah.
My luck smelleth to Heaven
And I am disheartened,
Therefore shall I turn my hand elsewhere
And become a Tram Driver.
For again I say unto you, that of all Pilots
I am the most unlucky,
Yea, d—d unlucky.

So distressed was he over his bad luck, and so sad was it to see one built for mirth so melancholy, that a small silk bag was made, a pebble from the beach put in it, and he was presented with this mascot, which he was told had come from Egypt. So great is the power of suggestion, that from that moment the hoodoo vanished. So gay did he become that on Guest Nights, after making one speech he would make another, and would make half a dozen more unless forcibly restrained.

Four Hun destroyers, after bursting out into the North Sea from Zeebrugge on the 30th of April, were on their way back when they were overhauled by Lofty Martin and Holmes in *Old '61*, about ten miles south-east of the North Hinder.

The North Sea was shrouded in mist, so at first the pilots saw only two broad white wakes. Then they made out through the haze two large destroyers steering on the same course as the flying-boat, and running at a speed of about twenty knots. They did not know at this time that they were Huns. Rapidly coming up with the destroyers from the stern, they were half a mile

BOAT ON PATROL. 230-LB. BOMB SHOWING ON MACHINE FROM WHICH PHOTOGRAPH WAS TAKEN

away when they were challenged with a green light, a single ball of fire shot up into the air, lighting up the mist with a sickly glare. The wireless operator in the boat replied with the proper recognition lights for the day.

The lather of foam beneath the bows of the destroyers increased, and the white tumbling wakes tailed out, as the engines of the destroyers were whacked up and the slim long ships thundered along at thirty knots. But the flying-boat was booming through the air at a good eighty, travelling two and a half miles to their one, and overhauled them as though they had been nailed to the water.

Immediately spurts of fire, followed by little black balls which opened out into nasty brown clouds, appeared in front of the flying-boat, and the pilots found themselves in the centre of a barrage of bursting shells.

Banking sharply to the right, Martin saw two more destroyers about a mile away, firing at him, ranged by the first two destroyers. He drew out of range and tried to get into wireless communication with Felixstowe, but failing, he returned to make an oral report.

Billiken and myself started out immediately to look for the destroyers. We saw no destroyers, but came upon a submarine of the U-C type twenty-five miles south-east of the North Hinder. She was just going under when we arrived. As she dived she made a sharp turn to port, and, as the bombs had been dropped a little short, she turned right under them. She could still be seen when the bombs detonated, apparently all around her.

So pleased were we with this little show that we steered a south-east course instead of a north-east course, fetching up at Margate instead of Felixstowe, and had to toddle up the coast to Harwich, where we arrived just in nice time for luncheon.

There was a great shortage of bombs about this time, for the number of bombs that had been dropped had depleted our store, There were only enough bombs left to arm one boat, so that each time a boat came in from patrol the bombs were taken off and put on the next boat going out. Uncle Pat, the

52

armament officer, went about praying that a submarine would not be sighted.

It has been said that the Admiralty up to this time had rated bombs supplied to seaplane stations as "non-expendable stores," and that the officer in charge of the Main Bomb Stores, when notified of the shortage, had replied: "Impossible! Felixstowe? Why, I supplied you with sixteen bombs two years ago."

When I first arrived on the station, Uncle Pat confided in me that he had just ordered a 1½ horsepower electric motor to run his lathe, for which his soul thirsted. From time to time, as the months went by, he would draw me into a corner and tell me of his latest move for he was a past-master in the art of intrigue whereby the motor was to arrive from London by the very next train. And then one day there was great excitement: he had word that the motor was actually on the rail. Finally, some considerable time later, a square box arrived at the Stores, and upon the lid being removed a beautiful new grey 1½ horsepower electric motor, with pulley-wheel complete, was revealed.

But by this time Pat had left the station.

And now we lost the first boat at sea. Poor *8659*, just handed over to the War Flight, was destined never to grow up and follow in the slip stream of *Old '61*. She was lost on her first patrol.

Monk Aplin and Rees had pushed off at six o'clock in the morning to look in the Spider Web, and should have been back in harbour at eleven o'clock. But they did not return. Wireless signals sent out to them were not answered.

The strain of sending out long patrols and waiting for the pilots to come back is almost greater than flying on them. I stood on the slipway with an ear cocked to catch the first faint beat of the engines.

I ran over in my mind all the possibilities.

Petrol: yes, the tanks had been filled. Engines: perhaps it would have been better to have changed the spark plugs in the port engine as the revolutions had not been quite good enough. Controls: they had just been overhauled, but the aileron control-wire, with the two broken strands at the fair-lead, had not been renewed owing to press of work. Hull: leaking slightly, but nothing to worry about even if the boat came down at sea. Wind: the patrol was not too long for the wind blowing. And so on, and so on.

I followed the boat round the Web in my mind and wondered where she had come down and why, or whether she had run into a crowd of winged Huns.

I telephoned to the pigeon loft and warned them. A speedy messenger was standing-by in the wireless hut, for at this time there was no telephone. The lookout man on top of No. 1 Shed had answered my questions in the same way many times. The seaplane and wireless stations up and down the coast had been warned.

And then I took a piece of paper and worked out a little calculation like this

$$32)215(6$$
$$192$$
$$\overline{} \qquad 6 \text{ hours } 40 \text{ minutes}$$
$$23$$

The engines used thirty-two gallons of petrol an hour and the boat carried two hundred and fifteen gallons in her tanks. She could stay in the air for six hours and forty minutes, and as she had left at six o'clock she would have to come down at half-past twelve through lack of fuel.

At twelve o'clock a little knot of anxious pilots were gathered on the slipway. I ordered two boats to be got ready and turned to the chart to work out probabilities and possibilities for the coming search. At half-past twelve, as the requests for information up and down the coast had drawn blank, two boats were boomed out to the Spider Web, and the Senior Naval Officer, Harwich, was asked to notify all destroyers.

When The Monk was out on the Web eighty miles from Felixstowe one of his engines began to give trouble. He turned for home, which he should have reached in an hour and a half, but at the end of this time he could see no land. As a matter of fact he was off his course and was flying more or less parallel with the coast, but out of sight of it. He shoved along, his failing engine gradually getting worse and worse, and his petrol tanks becoming exhausted.

His main petrol tanks finally gave out and he flew on his gravity tank, which contained sufficient petrol for forty minutes. He had just made up his mind that he would have to land through lack of fuel when he sighted a group of trawlers near the Haisboro' lightship, and, on his last teaspoonful of petrol, reached them. They were working over a shoal. A thirty-knot wind was blowing, and a heavy breaking sea, with steep crests, was running. As the boat touched the water it was thrown into the air and came down again on one wing. The seas tore off a wing-tip and a wing-tip float, and as the boat yawed, burst across her in a smother of white foam.

A trawler came alongside, and the pilots shouted to the skipper and asked for assistance. But the skipper, to their astonishment, bawled through a megaphone——

"I won't rescue any d—d Huns."

And then the pilots remembered that two trawlers had been sunk a few days before by a submarine. They shouted to the skipper that they were English, but he replied——

"If you're English, give us a sight of the Union Jack."

Flying-boats do not carry a flag, but the skipper would not be convinced. The fins of the boat had been damaged and the water was pouring in. The bilge pump could not keep the leaks under. When the boat was in a sinking condition The Monk thought of throwing across his naval cap, and when the skipper had fished it out of the water and examined it, he put a dingey out and took off the crew. An attempt was made to salve the boat, but without success, and she was a total loss.

Aplin, known as The Monk, because of the way his hair grew, or rather, did not grow, received a severe blow, when landing, on the identical spot from which he took his nickname, and never flew on patrol again, turning over to school work, at which he made a great success. And so ended April and the first eighteen days of the War Flight.

CHAPTER 3

The Phantom Flight

ONE

To appreciate the work of the flying service, it must be remembered that the pilot in the machine is only the spearhead of the weapon, and behind the spearhead must be a stout and reliable haft, so that the business end can be driven home with full effect.

The helve of the haft consists of the carpenters who true-up, inspect, and repair the machines; the engineers who clean, test, and keep the engines in order; the armourers who adjust the bombs and machineguns; and the working party who push about the boats and fill the tanks with petrol.

These men constantly worked against time at night, for long periods at a stretch, frequently rocking on their feet with fatigue, engaged on work which had to be done honestly and without mistake, for on it depended the lives of the crew, the safety of valuable material, and the success of the operations.

In the popular mind all work done by the flying service seems to be credited to the pilot, and the work of the men behind him gets overlooked work which is hard and exacting, and with little honour and reward. Owing to the shortage of machines, and the booming out of patrols in the summer months from three in the morning till ten o'clock at night, the men were driven at high pressure.

On the afternoon of the last day of April the Engineer Chief reported that the engines of one of the boats had to come out and be replaced. It was a job that usually had taken four or five days. The bomb-gears had to be stripped, the wings unshipped, the petrol piping and water connections cast adrift, and the engines whipped out. And then the whole process had to be reversed. But the tom-tom was beaten, a War Council of the four Chiefs held, and in the grey misty twilight before dawn next morning the boat was rolled out on the concrete to have her new engines tested, the men who had shoved the work through in the fierce stabbing of the blazing yardarm groups, standing about her, pallid, drooping, and haggard.

Two hours later she took the air.

'Twas May-day, and the happy pilots, Perham and Tiny, went off in her to look in the Spider Web. They were out past the North Hinder intently sweeping the horizon for signs of Fritz, when the engineer passed forward to them a signal pad, on which was scrawled——

"Sir, a float seaplane on our tail."

Perham popped up through the front cockpit like a Jack-in-the-box, and looked back. He saw a large and nasty-looking twin-engined machine right behind, and the smoke of tracer bullets lacing the air. On his frantic signals, Tiny shoved forward the controls, and dived for the water at a rate of knots. Just above the surface be made a sharp right-hand turn.

The Hun dived after them, all guns going, but failed to get a burst home. He flashed past when the boat changed direction. Having lost the advantage of surprise, the Hun pilot carried straight on, and quickly disappeared at high speed towards Zeebrugge, both propellers rotating briskly.

This Boche, when he got back to his base, must have told tall tales of the encounter; he was finally interned in Holland, where he was met by Perham, who unfortunately also became a guest of the same neutral country some time later. The flying-boats were painted a light grey, and the enemy pilot was spreading the pleasing report that it was no use attacking them, as they were made of armoured steel. He knew this, he said, because he had attacked one at close quarters, and had seen his bullets bouncing off. As a matter of fact, a careful examination of the boat failed to bring to light any traces of bullet holes.

Retribution fell upon us on this day for the loss of *8659*, for it was found that she should have been sent to the seaplane station at Killingholme, and sundry unjust people, accusing us of performing the act of hot-stuffing, demanded one of the War Flight's precious boats in *lieu* thereof. Two "alien" pilots arrived and picked out our newest and best, a boat which had just been painted, provided with wireless, and fitted with all possible conveniences and comforts, and in spite of our shrieks of protest shoved her down into the water and flew her away.

Seven enemy submarines were sighted and five bombed during the month of May; the first attempts to convoy the Beef Trip were made, not very successfully; and the first anti-Zeppelin patrols were carried out.

The Beef Trip, as it was called by the pilots at Felixstowe, or the Dutch Traffic, as it was known officially, was a convoy of merchant ships which ran two or three times a month between England and the Hook of Holland, and was alleged by the aforesaid pilots to carry Dutch beef to England and English beer to the Dutch.

In the dark hours of the chosen morning fifteen or sixteen cargo-boats would gather in X.I. channel near the Shipwash, and would be picked up there by destroyers and light cruisers from Harwich. The merchant ships would get into formation and start across the North Sea. The keen destroyers, sharp as needles, would zigzag and throw circles around them, like a group of rat-terriers chasing a cat around a knot of old ladies. They did this in order to intimidate any submarine commander out pot-hunting. While the swift light cruisers, stately and imperturbable, would boil along well out on the dangerous flank, apparently ignoring the fuss and fury of the show going on near them, but keeping a good lookout in case a striking force of Hun destroyers made a snatch at the convoy.

At the Hook of Holland another fleet of cargo-boats would be waiting in neutral waters to be escorted back, and the whole circus would start off again for England.

The pilots of the flying-boats patrolled the ever-changing route the night before, in case a hungry Fritz, bent on sinking the beef and beer, was lying in wait, and the following day would provide an aerial escort for the convoy, looking out for submarines, enemy seaplanes, which might desire to lay explosive eggs on the ships, or Hun surface craft.

When attacking single ships Fritz endeavoured to close to a range of from three hundred to six hundred yards before firing a torpedo. But when attacking a convoy they fired at ranges between five hundred and a thousand yards, and sometimes longer, in which case they did not pick out an individual ship, but merely fired into the brown. They waited in front of a convoy until the ships were sighted, and then submerged, therefore the pilots in the flying-boats flew in great loops from five to ten miles in front of the surface craft.

As the Beef Trip plodded along at eleven knots, taking eleven hours to cross, the flying-boat pilots were sent out in relays, meeting the surface craft at various places on the route as requisite, and remaining with them until relieved. The relays were so arranged that each set of flying-boats was out for five hours and a half.

This work called for extreme nicety in navigation, in order that the boats should make contact with the moving ships at the correct time and position. At first the results were rather ragged, but eventually it became an evolution. The pilots were later informed, in a letter of appreciation, that before they took a hand in the game the crews of the destroyers and light cruisers were kept at action stations throughout the entire trip, but that, now the flying-boats accompanied them, half of the men were allowed to stand off.

Zeppelins from the sheds of Wittmundshaven, Nordholz, and Tondern ran regular daylight patrols outside the Bight and as far south as Terschelling Bank. They did their navigation by wireless, so their positions and courses were fixed by the English direction-finding wireless stations, in the same way as the German submarines were fixed. The euphemism for this method in the service was to say:

"We are told by the Little Woman in Borkum that *Anna* is at so and so."

Anna being the first Zeppelin, *Bertha* the second, *Clara* the third, and so on. But they were wily birds and hard to catch, their crews keeping a sharp lookout around and all about. The boats had to cross the North Sea to get at them, and they could out-climb a flying-boat heavily laden with petrol for the return journey. They could only be attacked successfully by surprise, and at first the boats had no success.

These Zeppelins kept a suspicious eye on what our light naval forces were doing, and occasionally dropped bombs on the Harwich submarines doing surface patrol on the Dogger Bank. But fortunately gas-bags roll too much for good dropping to be done from them, and their bombs had little effect. Sometimes they would wireless for sea-planes to come out and bomb our submarines, but as, almost up to the end of the war, the Huns used bombs which touched off and burst on the surface of the water, they had little success.

I blew over to Parkeston one day to yarn with a submarine commander about this. He put me into a big soft armchair in the wardroom of the mother-ship, placed a potent cocktail in my fist, provided me with a cigarette, and then we communed sweetly together.

"Remember the Fritz your fellows sighted twice last month on the Brown Ridge?" he asked. "Sent out an E-boat to stalk him. Caught him blown on the surface. Put a tin fish into him. Thanks."

He did not use many words but said a great deal. I asked him if submarine often stalked submarine.

"Talked to a fellow up from down south. On diving patrol. Saw Fritz on surface. Torpedo blew Hun commander out of conning-tower. Sole survivor. Seemed much worried. Finally opened heart. Warned our man to clear out as four more U-boats were working in immediate area. Said he could not bear to be sunk twice in one day."

"Please go on," I asked.

"Boat from here stalked Fritz. Fritz heard him—dived. Both went blind under water dead slow. Our chap felt Fritz scrape past under him. Opened everything. Made himself as heavy as possible. Drove Fritz down to bottom. Soft mud. Sat on him for twelve hours. Tide silted them in. Our boat nearly caught. Just managed to pull himself out."

I asked about bombs.

"Don't think much of bombs. Bombed by Zepps several times. Crockery smashed. Great enthusiasm, small results. Boats are hard to kill dead."

"Sometimes," I agreed. "But how about that U-C off Ireland? "

"Which?" he asked. "U-C's are minelayers. Double hull. Only one hatch to conning-tower. Vulnerable point."

"The one whose commander popped up right beside a trawler, found himself looking into the skipper's whiskers, didn't like 'em, panicked, and pressed the diving button. The trawler was armed only with a rifle for sinking mines found on the surface."

"Right," he cut in. "I remember. Skipper shot commander. Body jammed hatch open. Boat dived. Fished up two weeks later in fifteen fathoms. Valuable information."

"And all done," I chuckled, "with an ounce of nickel-coated lead and a pennyworth of cordite. We carry bombs weighing one hundred pounds, we are shortly getting bombs weighing two-hundred and thirty pounds, and will soon carry bombs weighing five hundred."

He was very polite but not impressed, until I added: "And we burst 'em with a delay-action fuse eighty feet down. The bombs dropped on you by the Huns burst on the surface."

He asked me how we took aim. I told him about the bomb-sight, and that at eight hundred feet the bomb-dropper should make one hit out of three on a visible target. And I added that the flying-boats did eighty-two knots to the Zeppelin's fifty-five, so that a submarine had less chance to get down.

"That's all different," he said. "Hope the Germans don't do the same. Life's getting harder and harder."

Later on he told me this yarn. "Life's hard. Nobody loves us. Ships fire first, inquire afterwards. Off Terschelling at daybreak. Suddenly saw Harwich flotilla. Didn't know they were out. Infuriated destroyers coming straight for me. Dived. Hit sandbank. Conning-tower showing above surface. Broadside on to flotilla leader. Right on top of me. Reversed one engine, went ahead on other. Swung round. Destroyer shaved past. Wash lifted me off. Slid into deep water. Depth charges dropped. Electric lamps and crockery broken. Much annoyed. Said so when I returned."

I had another yarn with him in 1918. He said: "On Dogger Bank. Saw Zeppelin. Later saw seaplane. Dived. Hundred and fifty feet. Bomb exploded eighty feet above me. Shook boat badly. Moved north eighty miles. Same thing happened. What's to be done?"

Two

Down on the sea boats are not easy to handle with precision. But I once did a little bit of seamanship of which I am rather proud. It is a trick I would never try to repeat.

Lofty Martin and myself were out together in two boats on the 5th, when we sighted a Fritz twenty miles south-east of the North Hinder. Lofty was nearer and went bald-headed at him. The commander of the submarine saw him coming and dived, but Lofty let go his four bombs just as Fritz went under. And then I saw that his boat was in difficulties. He got into a dangerous bank and into a steep dive, but gradually righted and landed on the water.

Flopping around above him, my wireless operator, leaning far over the side, tried to attract his attention with the Aldis signal-

DESTROYERS ON BEEF TRIP

lamp, but without success. The bow of the boat seemed to be down and the tail up. There was a brisk east wind blowing with a fair sea running, and I thought he might have damaged the bottom of his boat in getting down, So I cut my engines and ducked in beside him.

Taxiing across his bow, I asked what was the trouble. An aluminium casting, holding the pulley-wheel through which an aileron control-wire was led, had broken. It could not be repaired. The crew had all gathered in the bow to examine the break. And at that moment his port engine failed.

We were fifty miles from harbour.

Early in the war two boat pilots down at sea had been captured by a Fritz, so before we did anything further we taxied ten miles into a minefield in case the U-boat had not been damaged and came up to investigate. Then Lofty shut down his one good engine, put out a sea-anchor, and hove to.

A sea-anchor is a large canvas bag shaped like a cone. Its mouth is held open by a stout wooden ring. In the apex of the cone is a small hole. When the sea-anchor is put overboard at the end of a line, it offers resistance to the drag of the boat drifting in the wind and so decreases the rate at which it moves. It also prevents the boat from yawing that is, it keeps the bow of the boat to the sea and wind.

Lofty asked for tools; so I taxied behind him and came up alongside, laying my port wing behind his starboard wing. The boats were rolling and tossing, and it looked as though the wings would be torn off. With a loud crackling of spruce my port propeller shattered his starboard aileron. But a line was passed, and I quickly drifted astern of him and hung on there. Along this line were sent tools, a spare sea-anchor, and food.

It was now five o'clock, and we had been down on the water two hours. The wind had increased to thirty knots, and a considerable sea was running. Advising Lofty to repair his engine and taxi straight down-wind, I cast the line off and blew well clear of him. Then I dropped my bombs safe to lighten the boat, had the engines started, and got off the water after five tremendous bumps. My wireless aerial had been carried away on landing. With a makeshift affair, rigged up with a spool of copper wire from the engineer's tool-kit, the wireless operator could get no answer.

Once in the air I flew directly down-wind, and almost immediately fetched up at the Edinburgh lightship in the Thames estuary, doing the twenty-five mile journey in fourteen minutes. Here a destroyer was acting as traffic policeman, so I landed near her. In reply to an Aldis lamp-signal the commander sent a boat and I went on board, leaving the flying-boat riding to her sea-anchor. I gave the position of the disabled boat and the information that Lofty would taxi straight down-wind.

Back on board the flying-boat again I had the engines started. The sea over the shoal was high and steep. After a short run in the wake of a passing paddle minesweeper I hit a big wave, before I had got flying speed, and was thrown into the air. When about fifty feet up I started to nosedive towards the water. I felt that I was going to crash, and crash badly.

Keeping the engines full out and the control-wheel back in my stomach, I shot down towards the water. The steep angle was increasing my speed and the engines were pulling like mad. I just touched the crest of a wave, there was a flicker of white water, and I shot off again into the air. This time I had sufficient flying speed, and boomed away for home. I landed at Felixstowe at seven o'clock. The engines stopped through lack of petrol as I taxied in to the slipway.

Lofty, out in the middle of the minefield, repaired the engine and taxied down-wind. He had frequently to stop his engines and fill up the radiators with salt water, as they were leaking. But he kept on. At half-past ten o'clock he was taken in tow at the edge of the minefield by a waiting patrol boat, and arrived at Felixstowe at one o'clock in the morning.

The remainder of the month was hectic.

Hodgson and Bath bombed one submarine and sighted another on May 10th. Ramsden and myself bombed another, and Hallinan and Magor met three enemy seaplanes, on the 19th.

And next day Morish and Boswell did in a submarine from a height of 200 feet, but, arriving back in harbour after dark, crashed their boat.

Gordon and Hodgson bombed a submarine on the 22nd, and next day Newton and Webster had a brush with three enemy seaplanes, shots being exchanged but no damage done.

A boat working up the Dutch coast had one engine fail at the Maas lightship, and flew homeward for an hour and a half on one engine, finally having to land at sea twenty miles north-west of the North Hinder. It was found and towed in by a destroyer. The Navy people, meeting the boats at all hours off the Dutch coast, and realising that we were doing a job of work outside, were now almost affable.

School work was also in full swing, for a boat had been turned over to the War Flight for this purpose, and the first pilots in their spare time crashed around instructing the second pilots in the gentle art of taking off and landing a big boat an exercise which proved equally hard on the nerves of the instructors and on the bottom of the machine, as there was only a single control-wheel fitted and the first pilot had to give up all control to the pupil.

During this intensive work it was quickly found that the majority of the pilots could only stand an average of one long patrol in three days as a steady routine, and that if they went out oftener their work suffered. It was also found essential that they should be given regular leave at short intervals.

I was beginning to feel the strain a bit myself. At this time I was my own intelligence, engineer, carpenter, and slipway officer, looking after all overhauls and repairs, deciding the suitability of the weather, as we had no meteorological hut, and putting into the water and taking out again all machines, excepting when I was myself going out on patrol. I determined the force and direction of the wind by the look of the waves in the harbour, the actions of a flag, or the way the smoke blew off a chimney. There was no telephone in No. 2 shed, and I had already worn out a pair of thick-soled boots galloping to and fro between the slipway and the ship's office.

May was brought to a close by a gallant rescue at sea, which is well worth telling in detail.

THREE

Hissed on by the ruthless wind, sea waves possess a malevolent cunning whereby they search out any weak spot in a structure made by man, and so finger, suck, hammer, and tear at the members which are flawed in design, material, or workmanship, that eventually the whole fabric is shattered.

The innocent wavelets dancing in the sun, pretty and sparkling, and the huge black rollers, whose crests under the weight of a gale, before they can curl over and break, explode into spindrift, are propagated by the wind blowing obliquely on the surface of the water.

When waves are first formed they are short and steep, but if the wind continues to blow in the same direction across a considerable stretch of sea, their length and height increases, and their crests, on which the wind has the greatest effect, tend to drive faster than the main body of the waves and so break forward in a smother of white foam.

In deep water waves have no motion of translation that is, the particles of water do not move horizontally, but merely up and down vertically. It is only the waves of force, born of the energy of the wind, that move across the sea. In shallow water the troughs of the waves are retarded, with the result that they become steep, the crests break, and the water rushes forward with great violence.

Water in mass played upon by the wind is not the tractable element it appears when running through our pipes, contained in shaving-mugs, or filling baths. Thus, while a land-machine pilot, down safely with engine failure, has all his worries behind him, the pilot of a seaplane or flying-boat, down at sea, has all his troubles to come, unless the weather be fine, help near at hand, or his craft very seaworthy.

Everything seemed to be set fair for a fine day on the 24th of May when Flight Sub-Lieutenant Morris and his wireless observer went down to the slipway at Westgate, a seaplane station on the East Coast south of Felixstowe.

At the top of the slipway, on its wheeled beach trolley, stood their machine, a float-seaplane with a single engine. It had wings which folded back along the fuselage, when it was living on shore, in order to economise shed space. A party of men were swinging the wings into place and locking them in flying position. The two large flat-bottomed floats were made of brightly varnished wood. The bombs were slung on the fore-and-aft centre line beneath the fuselage, above and between the floats. There was a third small float under the tip of the tail, and behind this float was a water rudder, a rudder operated with the air rudder, but which was used for steering the seaplane when it was down on the water. It looked very shipshape; a small stock anchor, with line neatly coiled, which was shackled to one of the floats, giving the right seagoing touch.

When the machine was ready the wireless operator stepped up on the port float, climbed up a little wire ladder, and settled himself into his cockpit, where he had his wireless apparatus, bomb-sight, and machinegun on a ring. By standing up he could fire forward over the top plane. Morris climbed up after him into the control cockpit. He was in front of the wireless observer, for the crew of two in a float-seaplane sit tandem.

Morris, looking over the side, saw that everybody was clear. He switched on the magnetos and opened a cock in an air-bottle. A stream of compressed air hissed into the cylinders of the engine and turned it over, the pistons sucked in the petrol mixture, a spark fired it, and the high-speed engine began to run smoothly. He warmed up the oil, tested the engine full out, and then gave the signal for the chocks to be knocked away. The working party ran the seaplane down into the water. It floated clear of the trolley.

When the engine was opened out the tail of the seaplane came up to the horizontal. It leaped forward, planing along the top of the water on the two floats. As the pilot pulled back the controls it skipped along with only the rear edges of the floats touching, taking little jumps off the surface as it encountered the tiny waves. And then it was in the air.

After spending some hours over the North Sea, Morris started for home. He was feeling very hungry, and began thinking about his dinner with pleasure. In half an hour he would have his legs tucked under the table in the mess. Suddenly he heard the noise of his engine and knew that something was wrong, for a pilot is not conscious of the roar of his engine when it is running properly. It began to miss. The revolutions dropped. And within a minute it stopped and the machine had been landed on the water.

They were down thirty miles out to sea in one of our deep minefields. It was a very big minefield. It started from an east and west line a short distance south of the North Hinder and continued to a line running east just above the North Foreland. Of course there were no ships in sight and no chance of any appearing.

The sun was shining, and little waves playfully slapped the huge hollow floats. But what wind there was, was off the shore, and blew the seaplane farther into the minefield. The two men examined the engine and found it was impossible to make a repair.

As the day wore on the wind increased, as the wind increased so did the size of the waves. The seaplane lay head to wind, its long tail acting as a vane. All through the afternoon it went squattering backwards farther and farther from shore.

When the waves grew big Morris dropped the bombs safe and opened a cock in the tanks, which allowed the petrol to run into the sea. This lightened the labouring seaplane. But about four o'clock in the afternoon the sea was running so high and the wind was so strong that the machine was overbalanced backwards and the waves reached up and began to pound the tail-float. The necessity for a tail-float is the weak spot in the design of a float-seaplane, and the sea was attacking the flaw in the design.

Morris climbed out on the nose of one float and the wireless observer climbed out on the other, in the hope that their weight would balance the machine and keep the tail clear of the water. But the waves increasing in length and height, an hour later the tail-float was crashed and wrenched away, the long tail sank down into the water, and the machine gradually turned over backwards.

The sea having succeeded by attacking the weak spot, and whipped on by the wind, now leaped on the helpless machine and tore it to pieces. The pilot found himself clinging to an undamaged float, and climbing across it saw the wireless observer in the sea beside him. Seizing an outflung arm, after a long struggle he pulled his companion across the float.

The float was a long narrow wooden box. It was very strongly made of three-ply wood. It was smooth on three sides, but on the fourth side, which was the top, were two indentations to take the fittings by which the struts that fastened the float to the machine were held. These indentations, with the remnants of the fittings still attached, gave the two men a handhold.

The float fortunately was quite watertight, not having been damaged in the wreck. But it was very unstable on the water and rolled about a great deal, threatening to turn over and throw the two men back into the sea. For this reason they could not climb up on top of it, but lay across, half in and half out of the water.

Owing to the great buoyancy of the float it rode high, like a cork, and so passed over the tops of the waves. But every few minutes a wave steeper than the rest, or which broke at the wrong moment, would drive over the two men and smother them under a weight of white water.

All through the night they clung to the float, defeating the efforts of the hungry seas, which came up and up in an interminable succession and tried to sweep them from their place of refuge. Just before daybreak a dark shape passed them, which they thought was a trawler, but the wind carried away their voices and the ship passed on and vanished.

With the break of day the force of the wind abated and the sea went down. Morris, feeling in his pockets, found a small glass bottle containing a few milk tablets. This was the only

PORTE SUPER BABY TAXI-ING ON THE WATER

food they possessed, and with great prudence he at once decided to dole out the precious tablets in order to make them last as long as possible.

The first day dragged slowly to its close. On the second day, the 26th, the wind died away and a thick North Sea fog shut down, cold, clammy, depressing. Its clinging folds wrapped them about, both body and mind, for it destroyed their chances of being seen and rescued should any ships pass. They had no idea where they were. The fog lightened to a light mist on the 27th, the sun shone through, and they began to suffer from thirst.

They were now able to lie on top of the float owing to the calm sea. To ease their thirst they took off their boots and went for a swim. Getting back on the float, they found that their feet were so swollen that they could not put on their boots again.

Each minute seemed an hour, each hour a day, and the daylight seemed worse than the dark.

On the afternoon of the 28th the mist lifted and the sun licked up the moisture in their bodies, increasing their thirst to torment. Their swollen feet were painful. In the wreck they had sustained abrasions and lacerations on their wrists and hands. The salt water had bitten into these wounds and they were inflamed.

Hope suddenly shot through the heart of the wireless observer.

Low down on the horizon he saw a flight of float seaplanes approaching.

They grew rapidly larger and larger, and nearer and nearer, until they were right overhead. He pointed them out with great excitement to his companion, but the later could not see them. They were a phantom flight. The observer told the pilot how the machines were circling around, the pilots waving their hands and promising to send help. Then they would fly away, but kept on returning at intervals throughout the day. But no help came. It was heartbreaking. And then the night set in.

Early on the morning of the 29th that is, after the castaways had spent five nights on the float the sun burst through the mist, which rolled away, letting them see a clear horizon all around them for the first time. But there were no ships in sight. Also the heat added to their raging thirst. They were very weak. At noon the fog began to settle down again, destroying their last chance of being seen.

The two unfortunates began to take sips of sea water.

This was the beginning of the end.

FOUR

Felixstowe was shrouded in mist on this day until eleven o'clock, when it began to lift. It did not look very promising, but I ordered two flying-boats to be run out and the pilots were warned off to have an early luncheon.

Leslie Gordon and George Hodgson, the Heavenly Twins, both from Montreal, Canada, were told off for one of the boats. They had been boys together, had come to England together, had learned to fly together, had been on the Nore Flight together, and when they came over to the War Flight they asked to be allowed to fly in the same boat. Either was willing to be second pilot to the other.

They flew together for some time, but owing to the scarcity of good boat pilots and both men were extremely fine fliers of the first rank they were made to separate. At first they resented any attempt to give them each a boat, but finally saw the necessity, although they had their names bracketed as Duty Pilots and for leave, and usually managed to fly their boats in company. Hodgson had been a champion swimmer. He was a stout fellow, in more ways than one, and built for big boat work. Gordon was a long-faced, serious lad, not over strong physically, but with tremendous determination and force, and was a careful flying-boat husband. Both men were great grumblers, but also great workers.

The boats were put into the water at seventeen minutes after twelve o'clock and went off to do the Spider Web. As they shoved out into the North Sea the fog shut down, and one boat, when forty miles from land, turned back. On receipt of the wireless signal announcing this, Gordon and Hodgson held a consultation. At first they were going to turn back too, and swept around in a large circle, but finally decided to push on.

When twenty-three miles past the North Hinder the fog became so thick that they could not see the water and they decided to return, climbing to a height of twelve hundred feet, where they were above the fog. After making the North Hinder again they started in for Felixstowe, and were twelve miles on the homeward stretch when they sighted, through a break in the fog, something on the water.

Spiralling down to six hundred feet they saw two men on an upturned float.

Winding in the aerial they came down to fifty feet and flew directly over the wreckage, and observed, from their attitudes, that the two men on it were in urgent need of assistance. They also observed that a strong wind had begun to blow and a heavy sea was running. Climbing to a thousand feet they let out the aerial and sent in a signal to the station giving their position, in case anything should happen to them. Then, in spite of the heavy sea, Gordon landed close beside the float.

With the waves bursting in spray over the bows of the boat she was taxied up to the wreckage, but the first attempt to take the two men off was a failure, as the engines being shut off at the very last moment, the strong wind blew the boat away from the float rapidly. The engines were started and a second attempt made.

This time Gordon taxied right up on top of the float. Two of the crew stood on the fins, one on each side of the bow, the waves washing up to their waists. But Morris and his wireless observer were seized, pulled up on the drift wires which ran from the nose of the boat back to the wings, and were drawn on board through the front cockpit in an utterly exhausted condition.

Gordon then attempted to take off. His 700-horsepower thrust the boat across the waves, hammering and pounding, but with the extra weight on board the boat was too heavy. He tried again. This time the waves smashed the tail-plane and tore off the wing-tip float on the starboard side. Also, owing to the pounding, the hull of the boat was leaking badly. The idea of flying back was abandoned.

The wind was blowing from England. The shore was forty miles away. The fog was thick. Two things could be done. Turn down-wind and run for Holland, making sure of a comparatively easy passage, or fighting home against the sea and wind to England a hard and difficult task.

Gordon shoved the nose of the boat into the sea and wind and began to taxi in on the water. The seas swept over the bow. The water seeped in through the leaks. The bilge pump, kept going constantly, one man's job, could not keep the rising water under. As the wind-driven petrol pumps would only work when the machine was in the air, one man had to keep the petrol hand-pump going to feed the engines.

Seas bursting over the lower planes were whirled up into the propellers and thrown back over the engines. They were white with the salt; but they kept running.

The tail was nearly full of water from a big leak, but a bulk-head held it out of the main body of the boat, although she was getting heavier and heavier, and was crashing through the seas instead of riding over the top of them. The sledgehammer blows shook the whole structure.

Without its float the starboard wing-tip buried itself deep in the water each time the boat rolled, pulling itself out again with a shuddering wrench, which each time threatened to pull off the wing.

The two rescued men lay on the slatted deck of the boat and were given sips of brandy from time to time, and finally a little cocoa from the thermos flask.

So, gamely, the boat won on towards England.

Four hours after landing outside Gordon passed out of the fog belt and saw the Shipwash light-vessel, rolling and pitching, three miles north of him. It was a welcome sight. He was only a mile off his course.

He had travelled on the surface a distance of twenty-two sea miles a not inconsiderable feat of seamanship and navigation in a fog, with the wind that was blowing, the sea that was running, and the condition of the boat.

Here they were in the shipping channel. They saw vessels. Very's lights were fired as distress signals, and a cargo-boat, the *Orient* of Leith, bound for Yarmouth, saw them, came alongside, passed a line and took them in tow. Half an hour later they were under the shelter of the land and two armed drifters came alongside. The tow was transferred to H.M.S. *Maratina*, and Morris and the wireless observer were taken on board H.M.S. *White Lilac*, in order to get them ashore quickly for medical attention.

Gordon stood by his boat, which was now standing up on her tail, and she was brought safely into harbour, was repaired, and carried out many more patrols, being used, after she had done thirty-nine patrols in all, for school work.

Within two months Morris and his wireless observer, unbroken by their experiences, were again flying.

CHAPTER 4

Sticky Ends of L 43, U–C 1
and U–B 20

ONE

James the One was awakened before daybreak on June 14 by the ringing of his telephone bell.

The Duty Captain at the Admiralty informed him that the Little Woman at Borkum said *Anna* was at the Dogger Bank going south.

Consider the ringing of the bell the pebble dropped in the sleeping pool, and observe how the ripples widened, and ever widened, until they broke on the coast of Germany.

Number One rang up the Duty Officer, who slept, or rather did not sleep, with a telephone for bedfellow, for James the One always developed a thirst for information concerning station routine between eleven o'clock at night and three o'clock in the morning.

The Duty Officer came into my cabin and turned me out. I pulled on my woolly flying-boots, slipped into my shaggy fur coat, and jammed my naval cap on my head. This early patrol costume was a perpetual offence in the nostrils of Number One, and it must have looked odd to the stolid and sleepy ratings when I danced with impatience on the slipway, but it had the advantage of being warm and quick to get into.

I knocked at the door of Number One's cabin and entered, to find him sitting up in bed examining a squared chart of the North Sea. A squared chart is used when signalling secret information concerning our own ships and aircraft or those of the enemy. I was informed of the interesting peregrinations of *Anna*, and that twenty minutes before she was at X.Y.B. centre.

Passing out through the mess I took a look at the recording barometer, which was high and steady, and went out on the quarterdeck to look at the weather. The stars were shining, a light east wind was barely perceptible, and a thin mist shrouded the buildings of the station and the ships in the harbour. But it looked as though the mist would lift, so I crossed the quarterdeck to the ship's office, where I turned out the Quartermaster, whom I found asleep, wrapped up in a blanket, balanced in a perilous position on the edges of three chairs.

The Quartermaster, electric torch in hand, doubled over to the officers' quarters, shook the Duty Steward, put a match to the ready-laid galley fire, and called the Duty Pilots. He then turned out the working party, the engineers, and the armourers, and warned the wireless operator and the flying engineer.

By this time I was down in the dark seaplane shed, in which only a single police light was burning, stumbling about among the monstrous shapes of the sleeping flying-boats. The marine sentry, recognising me by my language, turned on the roof electrics and flooded the shed with light.

The working party filtered in stretching and yawning, and rolled back the sixty-foot doors. They gathered round 77, which stood just inside the doorway on her wheeled trolley. She was fitted with specially large petrol tanks for the job in hand. At the word they pushed her out sideways, jacked her up, removed the side way wheels, turned her nose towards the water, and handed her over to the engineers, who started the engines.

The armourers fitted on the machineguns and provided them

with special ammunition. The man told off for the purpose put on board a packet of sandwiches, a bottle of water, the five days' emergency ration in case the boat came down at sea, the Bed Cross Box and the pigeons.

The oil in the engines being now warm, the engineers opened out one engine at a time, the fierce slipstream from the propellers shaking the whole tail of the boat and whirling up clouds of dust from the concrete. A two-foot flame stood out from each exhaust pipe, and particles of incandescent carbon, burning red, were blown backwards for many yards. In daylight you cannot see the flame or carbon.

It was now just beginning to get light. An eight-knot easterly wind was blowing, but a thick mist lay in the harbour, a mist too thick to take off in. So the engines were shut off and I went up to the mess. Here I found Billiken and Dickey devouring eggs and bacon, and joined them.

Billiken, a lad from Sault St Marie, Canada, was one of the best boat pilots ever in the service.

There are only two kinds of boat pilots the good and the bad. In the spring of 1917 the good boat pilots could be counted on the fingers and thumbs of two hands, and throughout the year there were probably never more than twenty first-class men operating at the same time.

A good boat pilot is one who can handle his boat under any conditions, a mist flier, a stout and determined fellow; one who can navigate and trusts his own calculations; a tireless observer, who knows where and what to look for; a possessor of sea sense and seamanship; a man of physical stamina or nervous staying power; a man of quick and correct thought and action, but, at the same time, one who could endure monotony and wait for his opportunity.

And Billiken, short, stocky, and with plenty of energy, possessed most of these characteristics, and others equally as valuable. He was modest, keen, and never given to swell-headedness or boasting, the latter being unpleasant diseases which are apt to attack young boat pilots, for there is an exhilaration in handling machines of great horse power and in the flattery of, to use the term of an old naval surgeon, the long-haired things. Or to quote a flying versifier:

For I have known the freedom of the air,
Nor crawled on earth like some coarse, dull, fat slug.

And again:

Such subtle poisons as sweet women brew
Have stuffed my veins with fire and my brain
With fantasy, making this cooling earth
Seem paradise.

Dickey was a little button of a chap, but what he lacked in size he made up in bloodthirstiness. He was one of the best second pilots it is possible for any first pilot to desire. He was a good shot, a capable navigator, a fine observer, and always keen on going forward and loth to turn back. He always gave his first pilot the comfortable feeling of being absolutely trusted, and this is why I liked flying with him.

When his boat came down through engine trouble during a fight against heavy odds off Terschelling in 1918, he shot down a Hun machine that was attacking him while he was on the water. He then beached the boat, burned it, and was interned. While walking in a quiet street of a Dutch town just at dusk a huge German elbowed him into the roadway. He seized the coat-tails of the Hun and demanded an apology. The Hun swore in German not a pretty exhibition.

Dickey was small, but he carried a big stick, and when the stick came in contact with the skull of the German the latter fell senseless. Informing the police that a man had been found unconscious in the roadway, the little fire-eater obtained an ambulance and tenderly removed his fallen foe to hospital.

Such was Dickey.

The quarry these two pilots were crossing the North Sea to hunt was a Zeppelin, an airship over six hundred feet long. It carried a crew of captain, second in command, a warrant officer who did the navigation, a warrant officer engineer, two engineer ratings for each of the five engines, a petrol man, and six other hands, of which two worked the elevators, two steered, one attended to the wireless and signalling, and one repaired the fabric.

All these men had received a highly specialised training at Nordholz, the course lasting not less than six months. Also the deck-ratings and the engine-room mechanics were trained in aerial gunnery, and when at action stations the men not on watch were employed as machine-gunners.

Throughout this month there had been great Zeppelin activity over the North Sea, for early in the year the German military craft had been handed over to the German navy, and the best airships of the two services had been concentrated near the German coast at Nordholz, Wittmundshaven, Ahlhorn, and Tondern. Until May 1916 the Zeppelins had carried out their patrols at a height of a thousand feet, looking for our minefields and scouting for our naval forces, but in this month L-7 was destroyed by gunfire from a naval unit, and they were now, excepting on rare occasions, carrying out their work at a great altitude.

At four o'clock the mist began to lift; we went down to the shed, the engines were started, the crew climbed on board, and at five o'clock Billiken took the flying-boat off the harbour.

When he turned 77 out to sea and steadied on the course, Billiken saw below him through the mist, within the encircling arm of the harbour, the tall sheds of the station, the light cruisers and destroyers at anchor, the submarines nestling close to their mother ships, and the minesweepers disentangling themselves from their own particular crowded dock preparatory to beginning the day's work.

He then glanced back down inside the hull of the boat, and saw Dickey busy with notebook and wind-tables working out the allowances, the wireless operator fingering his box of tricks as he tuned in with his shore station, and the engineer going over his petrol-pumps. This was the eighth time he had been out on a similar errand, but so far he had not been successful.

As he passed out of the approaches to Harwich the mist

'77 IN THE MIST......

shut in; so he brought the boat down to five hundred feet, and fifteen minutes later he passed the Shipwash. This was the last thing he was to see until he sighted the Dutch Islands, and from this time on navigation was done by compass, dead-reckoning, and inspiration.

To a land-machine pilot a compass is an instrument in which he has no trust. It may show him the way over the lines and the way back, or it may not. It may apparently go mad, and swing round and round, or the north point may steady on anywhere but north.

But the flying-boat pilot has to rely on his compass. He uses a big one, and puts it in a place where it will not be affected by iron or steel; or if it is, and he cannot correct the error, he marks the errors on a card and sets it up where it can be seen. He understands variation, which is the difference between the true and magnetic bearing, and which varies all over the world, and at any one place, from year to year. And he can steer a course within two degrees.

When Billiken was over a big minefield well out in the No Man's Land of the North Sea, the mist thickened, and, just to make it more difficult, the sun, large and red of face as if with the exertion of climbing above the horizon, was on a level with his eyes, and made it hard for him to see his instruments.

After they had plugged along for two hours and fifteen minutes, frequently coming down to two hundred feet to pass under a particularly heavy bank of mist, Dickey, through a rift, saw the flat shores of the island of Vlieland.

Here course was altered, and at half-past seven they were off the island of Ameland. Now, sweeping in a twenty-mile circle, they headed back down the coast homeward bound. The mist was lifting in patches. At half-past eight they were off Vlieland again.

Dickey suddenly saw a Zeppelin.

It was five miles on the starboard beam, at a height of only fifteen hundred feet.

Billiken swung the bow of '77 towards the airship. He opened out his engines. He climbed straight for the Zeppelin.

Dickey was at the bow gun, the wireless operator was at the midships gun, and the engineer was at the stern guns. The Zeppelin was barely moving. Her propellers were merely ticking over.

They were now at two thousand feet, a thousand yards away from the airship, and above her. Now the lookout on the Zeppelin saw the flying-boat. The propellers vanished as the engines were speeded up. She moved forward. She swung away on a new course. Two men raced to the gun on the tail and the gun amidships on top.

Billiken dived on the Zeppelin's tail at a screaming hundred and forty miles an hour. He passed diagonally across her from starboard to port. When one hundred feet above and two hundred feet away Dickey got in two bursts from his machinegun.

He used only fifteen cartridges.

As he cleared the Zeppelin, Billiken made a sharp right-hand turn, and found himself slightly below and heading straight for the enemy. He read her number, L 43. Her immense size staggered him.

Then he saw that she was on fire.

Little spurts of flame stabbed out where the explosive bullets had torn the fabric, and the incendiary bullets had set alight the escaping hydrogen.

Pulling back his controls, he lifted the boat over the airship, and just in time. With a tremendous burst of flame a flame so hot that all on board the flying-boat felt the heat the millions of cubic feet of hydrogen were set off. She broke in half. Each part, burning furiously, fell towards the water.

The top gunner rolled into the flames and vanished.

Three men fell out of the gondolas. Turning over and over they struck the water in advance of the wreckage.

The remnants of the Zeppelin fell into the sea, and a heavy pillar of black smoke reared itself to the sky.

The crew of the flying-boat fell on each other's necks. Everybody crowded into the control cockpit. During the demonstration Billiken got the heavy boat into extraordinary positions.

Just in nice time for luncheon, at fifteen minutes after eleven o'clock, having completed a flight of nearly four hundred miles, Billiken brought '77 into the harbour, Dickey firing Very's lights and the handkerchiefs of the crew fluttering from the barrels of the machineguns.

TWO

That night the staff-room was full to overflowing when Dixie brought in the brass tray covered with cocktails.

The staff-room at this time was a small narrow place, so narrow that when anybody sat down everybody else fell over his feet. It was just big enough to hold, with a little packing, the heads of departments who were permanently attached to the station, and it had become their room by an unwritten law. But now all hands were crowded in.

Everybody was standing, there was no room to do anything else, and a fine of half a crown fell on anybody who sat on the arm of a chair, a rule enforced to preserve the integrity of the furniture.

The noise was prodigious. All were talking, nobody listening. A lad from up North had just finished telling me a yarn.

"The Orks are the limit," he said. "A Fritz ran ashore at half tide on a small island just outside Kirkwall in the Orkneys. The crew got busy and took all their ammunition and heavy gear ashore to lighten her and got her off next tide. It's a desolate place, the butt-end of nowhere, but an Ork saw them. He was sent for by the S.N.O.

"'Did you know they were Germans?' he was asked.

"'I thought they werena talking English' the Ork replied cautiously.

"'Why did you not warn the coastguard at the telephone?'

"'They might ha shot at me.'

"'Did you know you would have got a big reward?'

"'Reward! Hoo much?'

"'A hundred pound.'

"'A hunder poonds! If I'd knawn that I'd have rin like h—!'

"I saw him the other day," concluded the pilot, "and he hasn't yet recovered from his loss."

Number One, who had just entered, was saying to Billiken: "Well, young Hobbs, I suppose you are proud of yourself. . . ." Dickey was over in the corner telling Pat, Jumbo, and the Padre all the horrible details. Pat was interjecting at intervals: "And the gun did not jam." The Padre was saying under his breath: "Poor souls. Poor souls."

Leslie, Tiny, Spring-heel Jack and the rest were talking at a rate of knots, discussing whether Zepps would give us any further chances, or if they would now fly high. As a matter of fact they did fly high from that time on, airships which could not get above ten thousand feet being withdrawn from the operations in the North Sea.

Every few minutes a signalman would wedge himself into the room bringing a signal of congratulation.

Then the Chief Steward entered and announced to Number One: "Dinner is served, sir."

The mess was a long room running the full width of the building. The rafters and roof were painted a light grey, and the walls green, a shade of green which could only be conceived by a naval rating and mixed in a ship's paint-room. A long table ran the full length of the mess, crossed at each end by a short table, and the Chief Steward had contrived a specially fine display of flowers and decorated the table with large mats having navy-blue borders, the centres embroidered with gold eagles, the noble bird which is the emblem of the flying service.

Number One rapped on the table with a little mahogany mallet made from the wood of a flying-boat. A sharp silence. And then the padre said grace, "Thank God."

The dinner was good, our cook had been a chef at the Ritz before getting into uniform. Out on the veranda the ship's band played airs, ancient and modern. The members of the band were the only men in the ship's company that Number One did not begrudge letting off attendance at divisions.

The port and sherry decanters circulated. Two sharp raps on the table, and the King's health was drunk sitting, navy fashion.

A telegram of congratulations from Admiral Jellicoe was

read, followed by a long list from friends of the station; and then somebody sang out, "At 'em, Tiny," and the portly one in another second was on his feet saying

"Mr President, I beg to propose the health of Sub-Lieut. Hobbs and Sub-Lieut. Dickey...."

Immediately after the King's health six sad officers left the table and went to their cabins. They were the Duty Pilots who had to turn out an hour before daybreak next morning to go on patrol.

****

Spring-heel Jack told me during dinner that throughout the entire day the German wireless stations had been calling frantically to L 43.

THREE

We were very proud of our new flying office in No. 2 Shed.

It was just inside the big sliding doors opening out on the slipway. It had glass windows on three sides which kept out the dust and some of the noise. It contained a soundproof cabinet complete with telephone, a desk at which writing could be done, and with drawers in which to keep papers, and a blackboard on the wall for notices. The inside was painted white to reflect all the light possible, and the outside grey to prevent it looking dirty. It was exceedingly smart.

Also a pigeoner's caboosh was put up.

The pigeoner was a busy man he seemed to do everything but look after the pigeons. There were several of him, for he had to be on duty before patrols went out in the morning and after they came back at night.

If you mislaid your lifebelt you asked the pigeoner. He kept them. They were air-bags worn like a waistcoat, and were blown up by pressing a handle which punctured a cap in a small compressed-air bottle. Everybody out on patrol wore one. It was good joss.

He kept the leather jackets and trousers for the ratings, for the War Flight was short of kit and it had to be passed on from man to man.

The engineers drew from him their flying-tool kits, small wooden boxes fitted with all tools that could be used at sea, packed into the smallest space and totalling the least possible weight.

Besides all this he looked after the emergency rations, the ordinary rations, the Red Cross boxes, the spare sea-anchors, the jerseys for the ratings supplied by the R.N.A.S. Comforts Fund, the cameras; and in his spare time he acted as messenger, being summoned to the Flight Office by one tap of the ship's bell. A lazy Duty Officer had fitted up a string, whereby, sitting at the desk inside the office, he could ring the bell outside.

He also looked after the pigeons. Large wicker baskets were brought down each morning from the military loft in Felixstowe town. While on the station the birds were watered but not fed. When a boat was going out the pigeoner put two of them in a basket with two compartments and two lids and placed them on board, well up from the bottom, as petrol fumes made them stupid. Each pigeon had a tiny aluminium receptacle clipped to its leg to hold the message, and a ring with its number, so that it could be identified if it came back without a signal. The naval Huns usually released the pigeons without messages when they captured one of our seaplanes, sometimes turning the holder upside down.

Pigeons cannot fly in mist or when it is dark, and have to be specially trained to fly over the sea, two squeakers, as the young birds are called, being taken out in each boat for training. And sometimes they refused to fly in daytime, perching when released on some part of the machine. When they did return punishment quickly followed. Birds which refused to do their duty had their commissions cancelled and were killed and eaten.

But they did great service.

An aeroplane and a flying-boat crossed from Yarmouth to Terschelling. The aeroplane tried to attack a Zeppelin and received a bullet in the radiator, whereupon it had to land in the sea. The flying-boat rescued the crew, but was damaged in doing so and could not get into the air again. Two pigeons were

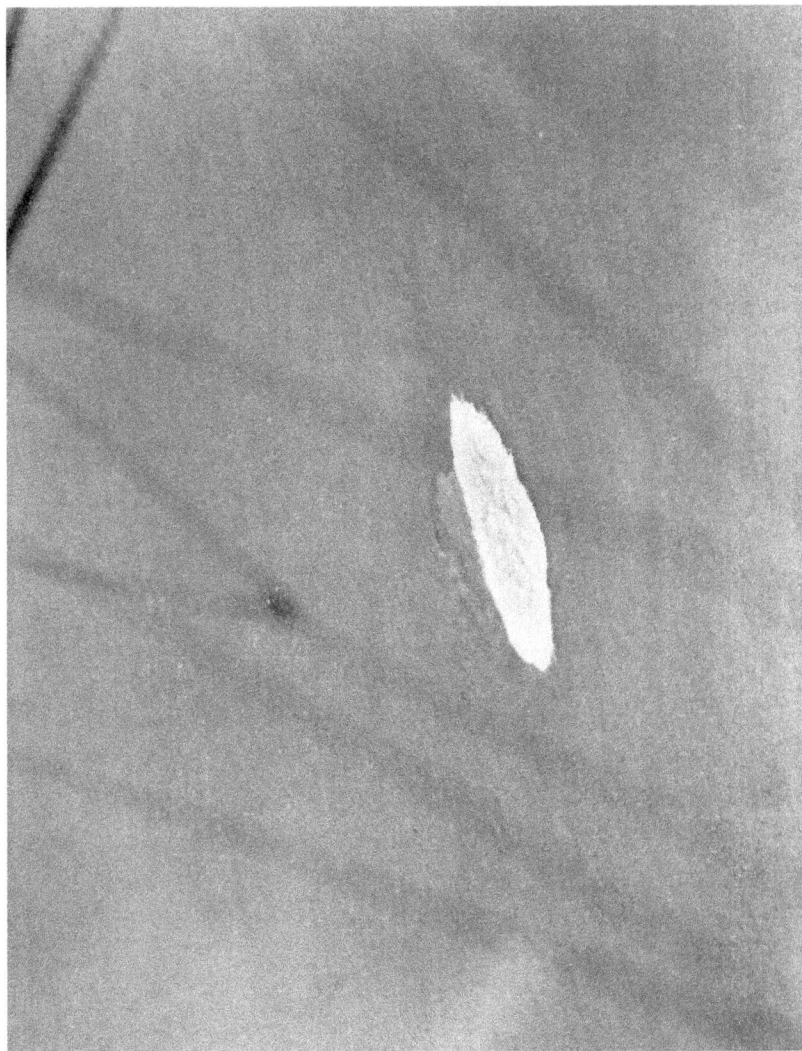

BOMBS BURSTING OVER SUBMARINE

released. One perished. The other, a great-hearted bird, battled home against a head wind and fell dead with exhaustion on the slipway. The message it carried saved the lives of the seven men who had been out in the disabled boat for four days.

During May, beside bringing down the L 43, the War Flight sighted eight enemy submarines and bombed three.

Morrish and Young, driven off their course by heavy rain-squalls and low clouds on the 9th, passed over an enemy submarine on the Schouen Bank, but as they did not know where they were at the time and could not identify it, they passed on, making the English coast near Dover. Two days later Gordon and Thompson presented one of our new two hundred and thirty pound bombs to a Fritz.

On the same day Dickey and myself, when peacefully booming out to the North Hinder, ran into six winged Huns. Much to the disgust of Dickey, who wanted to eat 'em alive, I dodged the enemy in the mist and carried out the patrol.

But now our activities were curtailed and the War Flight came in for a tremendous straffing.

A Senior Naval Officer from another area on a visit to the station asked to be taken out on patrol. He was boomed out on the Spider Web by Tiny, surprised a submarine on the surface, and dumped on it four one hundred pound bombs before it could submerge.

The Naval Officer arrived back in the harbour safely and departed to his own place, well pleased.

But that night the telephone bell rang and we were informed that one of the Harwich submarines, which was due, had not re-turned. Tiny's hoodoo was apparently on the job again. He was sent for and carpeted, and straffed for taking out a Naval Officer from another area, and while doing so, bombing and sinking one of our own submarines.

The War Flight was straffed and forbidden to search the Spider Web, and was given instead the task of flying up and down the shipping channel within smelling distance of the land. The pilots were tremendously bored.

And then five days later the E boat came limping in between the guard-ships at the boom. She was damaged, but not damaged by bombs. She had not been anywhere near where the bombs had been dropped, but had found trouble while poking her inquisitive nose into some of Germany's secret affairs.

But for some days the flying-boats flopped up and down the shipping channel, seeing nothing and accomplished nothing, until June the 28th. Their release was celebrated by Mackenzie and Dickey bombing a Fritz from four hundred feet ten miles west of the North Hinder.

FOUR

The U-C 1 pushed out from Zeebrugge harbour on July 23.

She was dirty as to paint, rust streaks disfigured her sides, and she was not a pretty object to look at in the bright sunshine.

But she was not really a wicked submarine, as she did not sink passenger liners or hospital ships with torpedoes or gun fire, but only laid mines, which is a legitimate act of war.

She was a hundred and eleven feet long, and was the sole survivor, but one, of fifteen similar boats. She carried twelve mines in four vertical tubes forward of her conning-tower.

Her Commander passed the North Hinder and pushed on towards England, running on the surface across our deep minefield. When in sight of the shipping channel he dived and worked his way right into the approaches to Harwich. He was a bit early, for it was still daylight, and he liked to lay his mines at high water, as this gave him a greater depth for diving.

He loafed along at two knots, thirty feet under the surface, with his periscope twelve inches above water, keeping a sharp lookout for trouble. Presently he saw a fleet of minesweepers working in the distance, and creeping cautiously closer, observed that they were sweeping in an area between four bright-green buoys, marking off the corners of a large parallelogram. Consulting the chart supplied by his intelligence department, he saw that the trawlers were sweeping in the emergency war channel.

The minesweepers were working in pairs, travelling abreast

and some distance apart. Each trawler towed a kite at the end of a wire cable. The heavy wooden kite was V-shaped and sank under the surface to the required depth when towed. Between the two kites was a wire rope. It had chains attached to it, so that it dragged on the bottom, and rollers, so that it would not foul. In the bight of the wire was a serrated portion. The idea was to catch the mooring cable of any mine on the wire and saw it in two on the serrations. The mine would then rise to the surface and could be destroyed by rifle fire.

The Commander of U–C 1 told his second in command that these preparations clearly meant that the Harwich Light Forces were going to take a burst out to sea, and that he intended to lay a line of mines across their path.

At dusk the trawlers packed up and boiled off for home at top speed. The German Commander watching them said: "It is easy to see that they are burning Government coal."

Just before high tide the U–C 1 entered the parallelogram inside the four green buoys, still under water. She was a third of the way across when a sharp order was given, a lever was pulled, and a mine left one of the tubes.

The complete mine consisted of two parts, the warhead and the sinker.

As it left the submarine it slowly sank to the bottom and rested on its sinker, for in the warhead was an air chamber which kept it right end up.

A slow spring, automatically released when the mine left the tube, began to move a lever, and at the end of five minutes it pulled back a catch and released the warhead from the sinker.

The air chamber in the warhead caused it to rise. As it rose it unwound the mooring cable from a reel in the sinker. It rose to within eight feet of the surface and then stopped. A hydrostatic valve had operated a catch which stopped the reel unwinding. The valve could be set to hold the warhead at any depth under the surface required.

The pull of the warhead on the mooring cable closed an electric switch, and the mine was ready for business.

In accordance with The Hague Convention a switch was fitted to the mine, which would open, rendering it harmless, if the warhead broke away from the cable; but it had been carefully put out of action before the mine had been put in its tube.

The Commander of the U-C 1 crossed the parallelogram and laid all his mines at close intervals. His work finished, he slipped off toward the open sea, thinking with satisfaction of his row of mines with their ugly warty heads swaying to the tide below the surface of the water.

He pictured the Harwich flotilla coming out in line ahead, a light cruiser leading, her four hundred and thirty-six feet of slim grey length driven through the water by her forty-thousand horse power. He thought of her 3-inch protective plating, but this he knew only went two and a half feet below her waterline. He gloated over her armament two 6-inch guns, six 4-inch guns, and one 4-inch high angle anti-aircraft gun all useless when pitted against his mines.

He saw her in his mind's eye touch a mine. It rolled along her side. The soft metal protruding horns were bent. The glass tubes inside them were broken. The liquid in the tubes fell into cups in which were two solid elements of an electric battery. A current was generated. The exploder was detonated, and the charge of high explosive went off with a chattering crash.

But all that would happen tomorrow. He was well pleased with himself as he slipped along.

How could he know that the emergency war-channel had been shifted, that the four green buoys had been laid there for his special benefit, that the minesweeping was a bluff, and that his successor to the job of minelayer-in-extraordinary to the Harwich Light Forces would in his turn discover the green buoys, blunder into the mines intended for the light cruiser, and so depart this life.

Next morning he brought his boat to the surface this side of the North Hinder, and started for home. There was a light mist, no wind, and everything appeared ormolu.

But behind him at Felixstowe Commander Porte, who was

back on the station for a short time, had determined to lead out a patrol of five flying-boats a greater number than had ever been out together. It strained the resources of the War Flight, but five machines were finally shoved down the slipway into the water. Commander Porte was leading in F 2 C, his latest experimental boat, piloted by Queenie Cooper, the test pilot.

The five boats fluttered around in the water, each getting into its correct position in the formation, and then, at the signal from the leading machine, all had their engines opened out at the same time.

They boiled down the harbour, leaving five white streaks behind them, got into the air and pushed off for the Spider Web. Many times later on flights of an equal number of boats were got away easily, but this was the first time, and a sigh of relief and admiration went up from all hands on the slipway. It was a fine sight.

The formation passed the Ship wash, passed the North Hinder, and then, at ten minutes to eleven o'clock, the Commander of U-C 1 tried to dive.

He was too late.

Ginger Newton and Trumble dropped two two-hundred and thirty-five bombs on him from five hundred feet. Commander Porte and Queenie dropped two similar bombs. Cuckney and Clayton dropped one bomb. And the other two boats stood by ready.

But the career of U-C 1 was ended.

There was oil on the surface and a little white spot on the water, where a long string of silver bubbles, coming up and up, were breaking gently.

The water was twenty-four fathoms deep.

A fathom is six feet.

One of the boat pilots, curious to see what the bubbles looked like at close quarters, landed, but was unable to find the spot. Once in the air again he could see the bubbles easily.

But the whole of July was a good month. The pilots flew on eighty-nine patrols, and did sixteen thousand four hun-

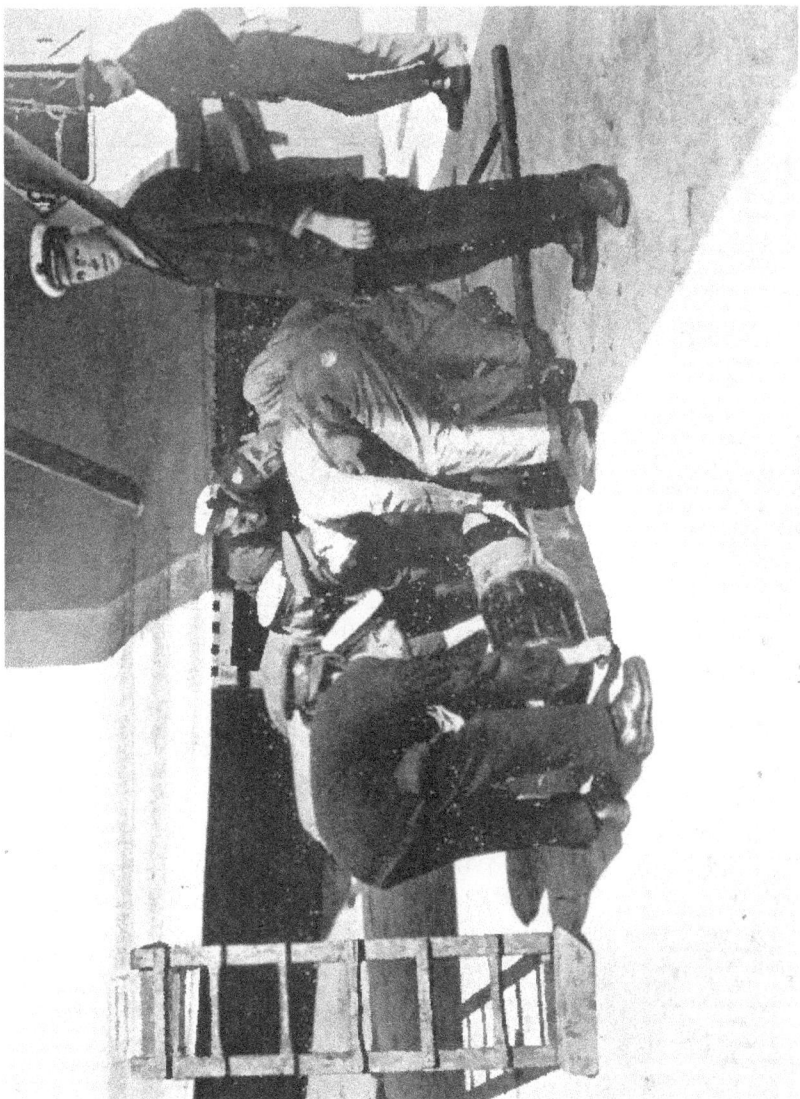

LIFTING 230-LB. BOMB INTO PLACE

dred and thirty sea miles. Twenty-five patrols were carried out, drawing blank, and then Puff Mackenzie and Dickey met up with a Zeppelin.

It was just after sighting twelve German destroyers, navigating along in close formation, that they saw the airship. Her crew saw the flying-boat coming at the same time. She altered course and went up through the clouds like an express elevator.

Holding on the same course as the Zeppelin, and climbing through the clouds for twenty minutes, Mackenzie burst up into the sunshine above and found the enemy still ahead of and slightly above him. There was great activity in the gondolas of the airship; and presently sand-ballast began to pour out, and she got to a height of eleven thousand feet when the flying-boat was at nine thousand. She had gained a bit of distance while climbing.

But now the coast had been crossed.

All sorts of odds and ends were thrown out of the gondolas, and the airship finally got to thirteen thousand five hundred feet. The flying-boat was at eleven thousand, just behind her; but it could climb no higher, being heavily laden with petrol for the return journey.

They were now thirty miles inland, and over two hundred miles from home, so the chase was broken off. As the boat turned round the disappointed engineer fired a few bursts from his stern guns, but the tracer bullets were seen to fall short.

Passing out over the coast the hostile destroyers were sighted again, and shortly afterwards Mackenzie had to land because of petrol pump trouble. The package of sandwiches was found and the thermos flask opened, and while the crew had a snack the petrol pumps were repaired. Twenty minutes later the boat was in the air again.

At half-past two Harwich harbour was reached, the crew having been in the air for six hours and twenty minutes.

Dickey, the small and bloodthirsty, would not be comforted for some time for not getting the Zeppelin, although it was pointed out to him that for one so small he had given the Germans a big fright.

Beyond shoving out a Beef Trip and the ordinary patrols, things were quiet until the 21st, when Perham and Cuckney in one boat, and Hodgson and Ramsden in the second, met up with a Fritz on the surface five miles south of the North Hinder.

She was lying in wait to sink the beef and beer, for a Beef Trip was on for next day.

Two bombs were dropped by the first boat. The submarine dived. It came to the surface seventeen minutes later. The second boat was getting into position, when it again submerged and was no more seen.

It is probable that this submarine was damaged, as she came to the surface so quickly after being bombed.

On the following day seven patrols were boomed into the air for the Beef Trip, the greatest number up to this time put out in one day. Owing to the number of machines being overhauled two of the boats had to be sent out twice, each doing five hundred and forty miles.

It was quick work.

Between trips the boats were taken out of the water, cleaned and filled with two hundred and forty gallons of petrol. The four machineguns were stripped, cleaned, and assembled. All control wires and the structure were examined. And the engines were checked and tested.

When coming in from the first patrol on one of these boats there was a splintering crash. I thought we had been hit by a shell from a pom-pom. But a tray of ammunition had blown off the front Lewis gun and gone into the port propeller. The brass-tipped mahogany blades were turning at twelve hundred revolutions a minute, for the propellers are geared down, and do not turn as fast as the engines. The tray shattered one blade, the splinters shooting through the top of the boat, but the crew were uninjured, except for a few scratches. The engine had to be shut off, and I flew the boat home thirty miles on one engine.

Flying-boats can fly on one engine if the total weight is not too great. It is a question of weight for horsepower available. To enable the pilot to keep the boat flying in a straight line without undue strain, a heavy rubber cord is fitted on the rudder wires, which can be tightened as requisite.

During the Beef Trip Hodgson and Ramsden sighted a U-boat, which dived. It torpedoed a small Dutch steamer seven miles north of the North Hinder, which was seen in trouble by Hallinan and Brown. They saw two boats put out, the crew tumble into them, and the ship sink.

Shoving off to the Beef Trip, for she was not part of the convoy, they flashed the position by Aldis lamp, and the two boats were picked up by a destroyer.

Next day Bath and Keesey, and Tiny and Moody, made a presentation of four bombs to a Fritz in the Spider Web, and two days later Perham and Barker, on the way in from the North Hinder, surprised a U-boat near the Outer Gabbard buoys, and followed the good example.

The end of July coincided with the end of U-B 20.

She was on her way south-about to the approaches to Ireland, where her Commander intended to destroy merchant ships.

For this purpose he carried a 4.1-inch gun and five torpedo tubes, four in the bow and one in the stern. He had ten torpedoes.

His boat had a double hull, and was a hundred and eighty feet long. She could do thirteen knots on the surface. Therefore he was able to overhaul ordinary merchantmen and sink them by gunfire. He liked to do this, because he could carry more shells than torpedoes.

The U-B 20 was designed to dive very quickly. But this time she did not dive quickly enough.

Puff and Ball in one boat, and Young and Barker in another, met up with her ten miles this side of the North Hinder. Apparently the Commander never saw the flying-boats coming, as he made no attempt to change course or submerge.

Puff passed over him at eight hundred feet, and Ball dropped one bomb.

It was a long slim bomb, with an armour-piercing nose, and weighed two hundred and thirty pounds.

Ball leaned out of the cockpit and watched it all the way down. Unconsciously he held his breath, and time seemed to stop. And then he saw it crash into the stern of the submarine.

On the explosion the stern went down and the bow rose out of the water. It smacked down a moment later with a wide-flung splash.

Close behind the leading boat came Young. Barker dropped two one hundred pound bombs. They detonated just in front of the submarine. He saw that the bow hydroplanes were damaged.

The U-B 20 was now out of control.

She did figure eights.

She dived and came up again.

And then, after seven minutes of such evolutions, her twin propellers stopped, and she began to sink by the stern.

The pilots were now circling above their quarry at a height of four hundred feet. Puff and Ball obtained a second direct hit just in front of the conning-tower, and Young and Barker straddled her with two bombs.

She was much down by the stern.

Suddenly she stood on end, remained poised there for a perceptible fraction of time, and then slid down backwards and disappeared in a smother of white water.

The pilots were back in harbour in time to dress for dinner.

But U-B 20, her wicked hopes frustrated, lay at the bottom of the North Sea in twenty-two fathoms.

She had been killed dead.

August was a cold miserable month. Mist and fog shrouded the southern portion of the North Sea, and when there was no mist and fog, heavy clouds hung like palls low over the surface, or there were heavy rain-squalls and high winds.

Only two submarines were sighted, neither being bombed.

But it was a welcome stand-easy for the pilots and ratings who had been working double tides for four months.

CHAPTER 5

The Fatal Fountain
and End Of U-C 6

ONE

I was sunk a thousand fathoms deep in sleep.

Came a loud rap at my cabin door, the stab of electric light in my eyes, and a voice saying, "Signal, sir."

The messenger, seeing I was more or less awake, crossed the cabin and passed me a signal pad. Propping one eye open, I read——

"0348 Trout, XUB top."

"Thanks," I said, and the messenger vanished.

The signal was a wireless fix of a Fritz. Sitting up in bed, I reached for the squared chart, and examined it. The message, interpreted, meant that at forty-eight minutes after three o'clock that morning, September 3, a German submarine had been on the surface off the Goodwins.

The commander of the U-boat had reported to Germany by wireless. He was probably taking no chances in that vicinity, and would not have up his aerial masts, but would be using as aerials the two jumping wires which ran from end to end of his boat, passing over his conning-tower and forming a protection against nets, hawsers, and mines. He could therefore dive immediately.

However, it was not my pigeon; he was not in the Felixstowe area. So I switched off the light, turned over, and was immediately asleep.

An hour later I was sitting up in bed again reading a second signal

"0403 Trout, ANV centre."

"Wait," I said to the messenger.

The repetition of the word "Trout" meant it was the same Fritz again working wireless. I checked the positions and times of the two fixes on the chart. The commander of the submarine had come north about ten miles, and would soon enter the Spider Web. This was a different matter.

"Quartermaster," I said to the waiting messenger.

Jumping out of bed, I pulled on my uniform over my pyjamas, and met the Quartermaster as he entered the door of the mess. We stood together and looked across the quarterdeck. It was going to be a misty day. We walked down to the concrete, and looked across the harbour. Harwich, on the far side, a mile away, was invisible, but the big light-buoy, half-way across, could be seen.

"Can do," I said. "We'll take a chance. Turn out the hands; I'll call the pilots."

The weather had been so unpromising the night before that no early morning Duty Pilots had been warned off, so I hammered up Dickey for myself and Cuckney and Clayton for the second boat.

Cuckney was a stout fellow, who had been doing the two-trip-a-night stunt in carrying bombs from Dunkirk to Zeebrugge.

He was over the Mole one night at a low height in a Snider, a small float-seaplane, when his engine stopped. He pushed and pulled everything he could think of, but the engine would not start again, and he landed in Zeebrugge harbour. Searchlights blinded him, and the Huns let off everything that would bear.

The enemy then saw that his engine had stopped. Fire ceased, and two launches raced out from the dock to capture him.

They were right on top of him when he found the trouble: he had opened the magneto-switch with his elbow. He started his engine, and ran along the water in front of the launches. And then he zoomed into the air, followed by howls of disappointment and a hurricane of high explosives.

After working some time at Dunkirk, he felt a bit weary, and somebody, who mistakenly thought that flying-boat patrols were a rest-cure, sent him down to Felixstowe.

Quickly despatching breakfast, we got into our two boats, and pushed off for the Spider Web, Cuckney taking up station on my port-beam, a quarter of a mile away. The water was invisible, and as he was travelling at the same speed and in the same direction, he looked to me as though he were standing still, suspended in the air by an invisible wire. It was an odd optical illusion.

The farther out we got the thicker got the mist. We could only see any distance by looking up the molten pathway made by the reflected image of the sun on the little waves.

After sculling about for two hours, I balanced the boat on the controls, and quickly climbed out of the first pilot's seat. Dickey was ready, and popped in. I now devoted my whole energies to observing. Turning my back on the sun, I tried to pierce the blank wall of fleecy white.

I saw something sparkle.

It looked like a tiny fountain glittering in the sunlight.

Through the binoculars it showed up as a thin thread of water standing up all by itself in the middle of the grey, calm, misty sea.

Taking a quick bearing on the compass, I bumped Dickey out of the control-seat, and swung the head of the boat towards the fountain. I opened out the engines and shoved the nose down. Looking back, I saw that Cuckney had turned in behind me.

One minute passed, two minutes, four minutes. We had roared over six miles of sea, and still I could see the little fountain ahead.

Then I saw the submarine. She was a mile away a big grey

Fritz of the U-class, long flush deck rising toward the bows, conning-tower between bow and stern, two guns, one before and one aft of the conning-tower, and a straight stem. She was shoving through the water at top speed, about thirteen knots, and above her bow was the little fountain.

It was caused by a thread of water running up her straight stem and leaping into the air about five feet.

It glittered in the sun.

Two men were on the conning-tower, but they did not see or hear us coming. We were attacking up wind and down sun. We read part of her number, U 4?, but the second numeral was blurred.

Forty seconds after seeing the U-boat Dickey pulled the re-lease lever and dropped one bomb. He threw up his arm. I banked over and looked down. The bomb had detonated on the starboard side half-way between the conning-tower and the stern.

The submarine heeled slowly over to port. She stopped in her own length and began to sink.

Cuckney close behind me passed over. I saw a bomb burst on the starboard side right in front of the conning-tower. Her decks were now awash. An explosion occurred in her bow and several smaller explosions between the stem and the conning-tower.

By this time I was again in position, and Dickey dropped a second bomb. The bomb detonated about thirty feet away from her. Only the very top of her conning-tower was showing. And then she vanished.

The little fountain had been fatal.

Later on in the same day, in the vicinity where the submarine had been met, Gordon and Faux in one boat, and Hallinan and Hodson in another, were surprised from the rear by four enemy seaplanes. The Huns failed to get home with the first attack and sheered off, and as they proved faster than the boats they could not be brought to action.

About this time, on an absolutely clear day, with no wind, and in a boat with a well-tested compass, conditions under which navigation should be certain and easy, I was extremely surprised and annoyed to arrive over the position where I thought the North Hinder should be and not see her.

I buzzed round in a circle, saw that my compass card was apparently all right, took a look at my notes of navigation, compared my watch with the watches of the crew, and then felt quite helpless.

On straightening up the machine, and deciding to carry on the patrol, I saw a black speck on the water about fourteen miles away. Through the binoculars I thought it looked like the North Hinder, but it appeared more bulky than usual and smoke seemed to be coming from it.

Deciding that I had made some silly error in time or course I started off for the lightship, and found when I got near it that two tugs were lugging it along at about six knots towards the Dutch coast. It was being taken in to be repainted and over-hauled. The following day a new North Hinder, with the paint of the name very white and the red sides unstained by rust, was lying at the moorings on the shoal. The new vessel could be told from the old one by a small black ball on the mast above the lantern, a decoration which the original light-vessel did not possess.

On the morning of September 13th the Commander of a Harwich submarine was coming in from a four days' surface patrol outside the minefields in the Bight of Heligoland. He was one of the little lot of submarines who kept the continuous watch, day and night, for the coming out of the German High Sea Fleet. But he had been relieved, and had come down homeward bound past Terschelling, across the Brown Ridge, and when near the North Hinder, finding he was a bit early, he went to the bottom to rest.

He had been down but a short time when he heard through the E-boat's ears, which are hydrophones, the propeller noises of another submarine. It was on the surface and passed directly over him.

He was just about to give the order to blow the tanks and come up and stalk the Fritz, when two heavy underwater explosions shook his boat. He remained on the bottom. He listened for a long time. But with the explosions the propeller noises had ceased abruptly and did not start again. Finally he came up to periscope depth, took a good look around, saw nothing, and broke water.

He said: "I started in for Harwich on the surface. I hung out all my signal flags, let some of the crew stand on deck, and looked as friendly as possible."

While the E-boat was down at the bottom of the sea and the Fritz was up above churning up the muddy water with her twin propellers, a Beef Trip was threshing along on the surface, and up in the air, in the sunlight, were the flying-boats.

The pilots of the two flying-boats, on their way out to the Beef Trip, saw the Fritz on the surface and whooped over to investigate.

But the pilots of the first boat to pass over him, knowing our own submarine was expected to be in the vicinity at this time, and not identifying the submarine as a German, passed over without bombing him. They did not know that the Commander of the E-boat was lying snug on the bottom.

The Commander of the U-boat, who was out after the Beef Trip, when he saw the first boat pass over, gave orders to dive and waited for the bombs which did not come.

Billiken and Dickey, in the second boat, got into position when only the light-grey conning-tower, with a tumble of white water behind it, was showing. But they recognised him as a Fritz and let him have two bombs. They circled over the spot for some time, and finally saw oil coming up, which spread, and spread, and spread.

Things now moved rather fast. On September 15 Young and Barker bombed a submarine. Poor Young, almost at the very end of the war, was shot at the controls of his boat in a fight against heavy odds off Borkum. He landed the boat safely in spite of the terrible wound, and died before the boat had stopped running on the water. The rest of the crew were made prisoners, setting the boat on fire before being taken off.

On the same day Perham and Gooch had a brush with three enemy seaplanes, and Hallinan and Hodson in one boat, and Gordon and Faux in another, dropped four bombs on a Fritz on the 25th.

While on a Beef Trip with Watson on F 2 C, an experimental boat, I sighted an enemy submarine about eight miles away and hastened towards it at eighty knots.

The boat was fitted with a marvellous arrangement of brass taps, pipes, a compressed air bottle, and a long release lever. This was a gadget for dropping bombs by compressed air, which, according to its proud inventor, was to supersede the good old way of dropping them by pulling a bowden wire.

When over the submarine the lever was pulled, but the compressed air escaped with a derisive hiss and the bombs refused to leave the racks. The submarine submerged and a destroyer summoned to the place dropped depth charges, but there is a feeling that Fritz went off safely about his business.

The area was now being made so hot for Fritz that the Germans began to be convoyed up through it by destroyers.

Two

U-C 6 pushed out from Zeebrugge before daybreak.

It was on September 28, a thick day, a very thick day.

With her were three other U-boats, three destroyers, and two float seaplanes.

The Commander of U-C 6 kept station in advance of the other three submarines as they passed through the swept channels into the North Sea. He was fully blown. The whole flotilla rippled along at eight knots.

The U-C 6 was an old boat, the last survivor of fifteen similar minelayers. But it was his first command, and he was very proud of her. She had just been overhauled. Her paintwork was bright and the brass inside shone. True, she only had one periscope, but they had mounted a 22-pounder for him in front of the conning-tower, an ornament which no other of her class had carried. It was an old gun and not very accurate, and the recoil, when he tested it, had threatened to sheer the holding-down bolts or pull up the deck. But, as he said, it was better than nothing.

He led the flotilla up the coast of Belgium until he came to the Schouen Bank buoy, with its red lattice-work top hamper surmounted by a ball. Here he turned west towards England, along the northern edge of one of our minefields. At half-past eight o'clock he touched the southern arm of the Spider Web.

Suddenly, in the mist, only a mile away, he saw, six hundred feet in the air, a black body with wings.

At the sharp word of command his gun crew raced along the narrow deck to the 22-pounder. The breach was snapped open, a shell shoved home, the gun elevated, and then its discharge shook the whole structure of the submarine, which had not been designed to take the recoil.

The shell burst just in front of the flying-boat.

As the gun flashed the Hun Commander saw a long narrow object detach itself from beneath a wing of the boat.

It began to fall.

It wobbled slightly at first, but steadied.

It was coming straight towards him on a slanting path. Its black nose was pointing downwards and it looked to be travelling sideways.

In a shattering roar his universe disintegrated.

Partially stunned, shaking, and bleeding from a long gash across his scalp, he stumbled to his feet.

Passing his hand through his hair he felt that it was wet. He looked at it stupidly and saw that it was red. He could not understand.

He looked at the stern of his boat. The superstructure was torn away, and the steel deck, rent open like a sardine tin, gaped like a great lacerated mouth, the twisted metal turning up at the edges. His gun crew had vanished, where he knew not, but a pallid hand appeared above the surface of the water beside him, flapped feebly, made a few ripples, and disappeared.

Pulling himself together, and acting by instinct, he dropped down into the wrecked boat. At the foot of the conning-tower ladder he splashed into water. All electric lights were out. The interior was in darkness, except for the light from the conning-tower hatchway and the tear in the deck. He swayed unsteadily on his feet on the slippery deck, which sloped sharply down aft.

His crew below had been killed or stunned by the force of the explosion within the cramped and confined steel walls. A sodden mass, shapeless and horrible, washing against his feet, had been his second in command. The once orderly interior, a maze of intricate machinery, cunningly and carefully arranged by the sane intellect of an engineer, was distorted and twisted into an insane jumble. The bottom of the boat had been blown out at the stern, and he realised dimly that it was only the air in the tanks that was keeping her afloat. The chlorine gas, generated by the sea water mixing with the sulphuric acid in the storage batteries, bit into his lungs. The stern was sinking.

He felt sick. He had a great desire to get out of it all. He seized the lower rungs of the iron ladder.

A second heavy explosion shook the boat. Her stern went down suddenly. There was no light. He was thrown into the water.

The submarine sank.

Between the bow of the boat and the water was an air space. He flopped feebly on the surface in the inky blackness.

It was the end.

He let himself sink.

Only two minutes had elapsed from the time the flying-boat had been first sighted.

Up above in the mist were Billiken and Dickey in the flying-boat. They had pushed off that morning from Felixstowe in company with another boat, but the pilots in the second boat had found the mist too thick and had returned.

Suddenly, dead ahead, they had seen the U-C 6. As they roared towards her they saw her gun crew gather round the 22-pounder, and as Dickey pulled the release lever a shell burst just in front of their bow. The bomb hit the stern of the submarine.

Shells were now bursting all around them. This, to the pilots, was a mystery, for the gunners on U-C 6 were no longer at the 22-pounder. Then through the mist, and about a mile away, gun flashes were seen, and the crew of the flying-boat made out three submarines in line abreast firing at them. Behind the submarines were three destroyers, and behind the destroyers were two float seaplanes.

The pilots saw that U-C 6 was in serious trouble. She was down by the stern, the water was up to her conning-tower, and her bow was sticking up in the air. But they knew that submarines are hard to kill dead, often getting back to port after damage which makes the feat appear miraculous, and they were taking no chances.

Disregarding the shell fire, the flying-boat was taken again across the submarine, and the second bomb was dropped from a low height. It detonated immediately in front of the bow. With the explosion the whole structure of the submarine vibrated, she slid down backward under the water, and left on the surface, to show where she had gone down, a large quantity of blackish oil, foreign matter, and a silver cluster of breaking air bubbles, a cluster ever renewed from below.

Immediately on receipt at Felixstowe of the signal about the enemy destroyers and the sinking of U-C 6, flying-boats were shoved down the slipways and boomed out over the North Sea. Cuckney and Clayton sighted a hostile seaplane close to the water, but it sheered off and was lost in the mist. Young and Keesey found another enemy seaplane and chased it until it led them to two enemy destroyers. It was now very thick indeed, the mist changing rapidly into a fog, and while climbing to get well above the enemy in order to bomb them, the pilots lost their way and failed to find the surface ships again.

The following day, which was still misty, Gordon and Faux, while ten miles south-east of the North Hinder, saw a ripple on the surface, a streak of white water, and then the conning-tower of a U-boat breaking surface. It navigated along awash at about five knots. The pilots were at thirteen hundred feet.

Gordon dived to eight hundred feet, but Fritz had seen him coming and submerged twenty seconds before the two bombs exploded about the place he should have been.

It was thought that this submarine was at least damaged, for when the black circles left by the explosion of the bombs had cleared away, oil came to the surface, and by the time the pilots left the vicinity it was covering a fair-sized area.

THREE

October was almost the last good month of submarine hunting to be had. Four enemy submarines were sighted, but their commanders were keeping a good lookout while in the Spider Web, and only one was bombed, by Hodgson and Wilson.

The 23rd of October was rather a dirty day, with a falling barometer, and that unpleasant taste to the north-west wind which usually means trouble of some sort for somebody.

The Harwich Light Forces were off the Dutch coast looking for the elusive Hun, and sundry patrols had therefore been shoved out from Felixstowe. Two of these boats, Tiny in charge of one and Perham and Gooch in the other, boomed off at ten o'clock to look in the Spider Web.

On starting out Tiny's wireless operator let the aerial wire run off the reel unchecked, so that when it fetched up with a round turn at the end, the weight snapped off the copper wire just inside the boat. This made it impossible for him to send or receive wireless signals.

About twelve o'clock, at a position about ten miles south of the North Hinder, Tiny missed Perham's boat. Turning back on his course he searched for the missing boat, but failing to see it, concluded that the pilots had pushed off for harbour with engine trouble. But not being certain, he released a pigeon with a message, giving details, and continued the search.

After the boats went out the wind kept steadily rising. Wireless signals sent out warning the two boats were not answered. Messages were sent up and down the coast asking for news. Then a pigeon dropped down on the ledge outside its loft, walked through the swinging wires which rang a bell, and so into a little cage. The pigeoner, warned by the bell, went into the loft, removed the crumpled slip of flimsy paper from the carrier, and sent it down to the station.

Two boats were shoved out on the slipway and their engines warmed. Then Tiny came into the harbour and reported that he had been unable to find the missing boat.

In spite of the rapidly rising wind, which had now got to thirty knots, the quickly decreasing daylight, and the barometer that was falling with ominous persistence, Gordon and Faux, and Hodgson and Wilson, volunteered to go out and look for Perham. They pushed off in two boats from the slipway. The harbour was a froth of whitecaps, and the boats took off in a smother of spray.

Half an hour later a great-hearted pigeon came battling in against the quartering breeze carrying a message from Perham. Smoothing out the crumpled paper on the desk in the flying office we read the signal.

"Port engine crankshaft fractured. Good landing. Approximate position ten miles south of North Hinder."

I rang up the naval authorities at Harwich, informed them of the state of affairs, and asked for assistance. I was told that the Harwich flotilla had run into a minefield off the Dutch coast. The flagship of Rear-Admiral Tyrwhitt had struck a mine with her stern and the explosion had detonated a depth charge carried on her counter. She was returning to port at about two knots, with the sea that was running outside, and all available destroyers were required to guard the disabled light cruiser. However, help would be sent.

At dusk the two flying-boats returned. The pilots had made the North Hinder, had gone ten miles south and had searched a large area, but had failed to locate Perham.

And then a signal came in that the two destroyers sent to the position had been unable to find the flying-boat.

With the shutting down of night the wind increased in violence. In the open, when you stood up to it, it was like a solid wall.

The disabled cruiser outside was in a precarious condition, and many of her attendant destroyers had to leave her and return to Harwich, making heavy weather of it.

The wind got up to forty knots, fifty knots, and finally to sixty knots in gusts. The wooden mess groaned and protested beneath the heavy hand of the storm.

To a chorus of chattering windows, fierce spurts of smoke from the stove due to violent back drafts down the chimney, a chart was spread out on the Staff-room table and the probable course of the drifting flying-boat was laid out. All this, with the reservation in our own minds, if the boat would live through the gale. But it was at least something to do, and three boats stood ready to push off next morning, if required.

A chart is a representation of a portion of the surface of the earth intended to be useful to a seaman, and it therefore deals in detail with the portions of the earth covered with water. It gives the positions of lights and buoys, details of the sea bottom, and heights, magnetic variations, and soundings.

We drew a line on the chart from the positions, ten miles south of the North Hinder, where Perham had come down, towards the Dutch coast. This represented the direction the boat would drift owing to the wind.

The flying-boat, with two sea-anchors out, checking the drift, and also with weigh knocked off owing to the tossing of the waves, would probably not drift faster than three knots. Therefore the wind line was dotted off at three mile intervals.

Beside the movement due to the wind the flying-boat would move with the tide, so the set due to the tide was dotted on the chart at right angles to each three-mile mark.

When these dots were joined a wavy line was the result, a line first setting away from the main line of drift, then coming back to it, crossing it, and then setting away in the other direction. When the line got near the Dutch coast it could not be calculated owing to the curious currents, rips and eddies, set up by the low-lying nature of the land.

It was seen at once that the three boats would not be required next day. For Perham would drift past the Schouen Bank light-buoy about two o'clock in the morning and would be off the Dutch coast at Schouen by daybreak.

If the boat lived.

An extra heavy gust shook the building, and a great fall of soot down the chimney almost beat out the fire.

There was a general feeling of thankfulness and relief when the Duty Steward entered and asked if any one wished to give an order before the bar closed.

When, with a grinding crash, the crankshaft of his port engine fractured, Perham snapped off the switches and glided down to the water.

It was just twelve o'clock noon.

He saw Tiny in the air in front of him, roaring along with his well-found engines turning off a steady sixty knots. The clouds were rather low and the air at a thousand feet was hazy. Gooch fired Very's lights, but the crew of Tiny's boat did not see them, and boomed on.

The wind was blowing about twenty knots from England, and a bigger sea was running than the wind seemed to warrant always a bad sign.

The crew got out two sea-anchors to check the drift and keep the bow of the flying-boat from yawing off the wind. They fitted the covering over the forward cockpit to keep out water thrown over the bows. The bombs were dropped safe in order to lighten the boat. The engine was carefully examined.

The wicker pigeon basket was passed forward and the message-book taken from the pocket at the side. Two messages were written and rolled up. The wireless operator opened one of the two lids, took out a pigeon, inserted a message in the holder, shoved home the cap, and threw the pigeon into the air, head to wind. The crew watched the bird rise, circle twice, and start off for home. When it was out of sight the second pigeon, with the duplicate message, was released.

As the daylight hours passed the weight of the wind increased. The waves got higher, and finally their crests began to break. Riding to her sea-anchors the boat sat high and free. But as darkness set in the waves began to throw the water over the bow into the pilot's cockpit.

The petrol in the tanks, splashing about, gave off a heavy vapour which filled the boat, and this, with the pitching, added seasickness to the discomforts of the crew; for petrol vapour will make the stoutest-hearted seaman wish he had never sold his little farm.

Later on, blowing backwards through the darkness, as the force of the gale increased and the waves got higher, the flying-boat began to roll from side to side. The wing-tip floats on the lower planes buried themselves in the sea first on one side and then on the other. When they did this a great weight of water poured over the planes, wrenching, twisting, and tearing with all the leverage afforded by the length of the wing.

Perham thought of making an attempt to cut off the fabric on the lower planes in order to prevent the water from getting a grip.

Instead of this the crew took turns at standing, two at a time, on the lower wings, one outboard from each engine, and as a float went under the man on the opposite wing would scramble out on the plane as fast as possible, his weight tending to right the flying-boat. It was a hazardous expedient.

About two o'clock in the morning the crew saw the Schouen Bank light-buoy.

Here in the very shoal water, and with the clear sweep of ninety miles behind them, the waves were perilously steep, and the trough being retarded by the bottom the crests were breaking forward in a thunder of foam.

The sea-anchors carried away.

The boat, rolling and pitching, yawed first one way and then the other. Each time she got off the wind white water was driven across her from bow to stern. The crew were blinded and drenched. The wracking strained the boat, and she began to leak. The wood on the bottom of the flying-boat was not over a quarter of an inch thick. One man had to work the bilge-pump continuously, and the three other men in the crew bailed.

DUTCH SAILING-VESSEL PHOTOGRAPHED FROM A FLYING-BOAT

Finally they were over the shoal. The seas here, though big, were not so bad, as their force was somewhat expended in the shallow water.

With the coming of the dawn the worn-out crew saw that they were off the coast of Holland. There were long white sand-hills and green hummocks, and a lighthouse with a circular stone tower and a black gallery, and Perham knew that they had made a landfall at the Hook of Schouen. They were now being carried parallel with the coast by a strong current, so they made an attempt to start up the one good engine so as to taxi in to shore. After great difficulty they succeeded. Then they saw a Dutch gunboat, rolling heavily in the sea, approaching them. They shut down the engine.

The code-book, with its weighted covers, was thrown overboard.

The chart, weighted with machinegun cartridges, was sent after it.

The wireless installation was pulled out and tossed over the side, and the machineguns and ammunition followed.

Perham retained one machinegun.

The gunboat hove to to windward and gave the flying-boat a lee. It dropped a boat, which pulled down to them. The engineer and wireless man scrambled on board, followed by Gooch. They shouted to Perham to follow.

Perham was busy with the machinegun breaking a hole in the bottom of his flying-boat. So far no neutral or enemy Power had had a boat to examine at leisure. When finished, he joined the rest of the crew.

But once aboard the cutter, not satisfied with the way his boat was sinking, he seized a boat-hook and broke a hole in the 'tail, for the tail contained a watertight compartment.

The gunboat's crew made an attempt to salve the flying-boat, but were unsuccessful, as she sank. An attempt to grapple for her five days later also failed only the engines being recovered.

The cable announcing the safety of Perham and his crew was received at Felixstowe before seven o'clock on the same morning.

November had sixteen flying days, and one submarine was bombed by Tiny and Moody on the 3rd.

And now there comes a little yarn which might be entitled: The Pirates, the Birdman, and the Grateful Fisherman, and could be told thus:

A poor but honest Dutch fisherman had cast his nets and made a great haul of fish. His smack was filled to overflowing. He was exceedingly joyful, for he had a wife and three at home, and was expecting another. But, as he was thinking with pleasure of the pieces of silver which the finny spoil of the sea would put in his pocket, the sun was obscured, the wind blew, and the sea rose in mountainous waves.

When the wind abated and the waves subsided the smack was far from land, and neither the fisherman nor any of his men knew in what part of the sea they were.

While consulting with each as to what had best be done, the water near them boiled, a mysterious white wave broke along the surface, and a loathly grey monster of the deep heaved itself out of the sea and lay beside them. On its back were pirates bloodthirsty men, outlaws, a cutthroat crew the deeds which they and their fellows had committed having made the whole world shudder.

The poor fisherman and his men shook with terror.

The Chief of the Pirates, in a terrible voice, demanded that the fisherman come to him, so with great reluctance and many misgivings he put a small boat over the side, rowed slowly across, and was taken up on the back of the horrible sea-monster.

To him the Chief of the Pirates said in great anger, "We had a secret channel, of which none knew, through the dangers beneath the waters set for us by our enemies. Across the entrance to the channel I have found strong nets and cunning machines placed to destroy me. And you, miserable man, are floating over the very spot. Prepare yourself for destruction."

The poor fisherman protested his innocence of all knowledge of the trap, pleaded his wife and three, and the other that was expected, but it availed nothing. With a sorrowful heart he got into his little boat, and rowed towards his smack, thinking best how to tell his men of the fate in store for them.

But before he had completed the short journey he heard a roar in the air, and looking up he saw a huge grey bird approaching with two great eggs under its wings.

Fear now fell upon the pirates, and they incontinently caused their monster to dive, disappearing instantly beneath the waves. The great bird circled over the fisherman twice, the men on its back signalling to him, and then flew away.

While yet the fisherman and his men were congratulating each other on their narrow escape, swift ships, driven by fire, appeared. A strong rope was thrown to the fisherman, which he made fast to the bow of his smack, and he was pulled along the water at an incredible speed to the Island of England. Here he was brought before a man in authority, who had laid the trap for the pirates a man clad in rich blue and gold, and with a gold hat on his head. After answering questions for many hours, the fisherman was allowed to send his fish to the market, in the fabulously rich city of London, and received more pieces of silver than he had hoped for.

Indeed, if the one expected proved to be two, he could now easily afford it.

The grateful fisherman asked to be allowed to thank the Birdman who had rescued him, and one, Billiken, was sent for. The fisherman hailed him as his saviour, enveloped him in a long, odorous, fish-scaly embrace, and attempted to reward him by pouring out at his feet all the silver he had obtained for his fish.

But the Birdman in a noble voice replied, "For what little I did I want no reward, but please do not embrace me again; the emotion I experience is more than I can bear."

That afternoon the fisherman and his men set out for home, all the sails of their smack set and drawing in a fair wind, and English silver jingling in their pockets.

Two days before Christmas, Tiny and Moody barged into

two Fritzes, apparently in a great hurry to get home before the 25th. One of them was presented with two big bombs as a Christmas-box.

About this time, while tearing through the sea at full speed in the dark, the Harwich Light Forces bumped into a newly-laid minefield off the Dutch coast. Four destroyers were damaged and a cargo-boat sunk. As it was not known if the destruction was due to mines or a nest of submarines, an urgent request was made to the War Flight to send a flying-boat across to photograph the wreck of the cargo-boat, which showed above water at low tide.

The weather was impossible.

But every little while a request would come through by telephone asking for an explanation as to why the desired photographs were not forthcoming. With each repetition of the request the telephone became more and more impatient.

On December 27 Clayton and Purdy pushed off to try and get the photographs. It was a bad day. A twenty-five knot wind was blowing. They returned very shortly and reported

"Wind very strong, and visibility six miles from coast, nil. Had to turn back before even reaching Ship wash, as heavy clouds reaching to the water barred progress in every direction."

But this did not satisfy the telephone.

Clayton and myself pushed out at noon. It was a wretched flying day. The clouds were low, snow-squalls swept down before the north-east wind, and the air was bumpy. The heavy boat wallowed in the rough air. With the exertion of handling her I broke out in a perspiration. Although it was bitterly cold, I pulled off my short flying-coat and gauntlets.

We drove at seventy knots through low clouds and snow-flurries for an hour. But against the head wind we had only won forty-two sea miles from Felixstowe. Here, barring our path, was a nasty-looking bank of snow-clouds reaching to the water. We turned north to skirt them and look for an opening. Heavy gusts shook the boat: she rolled from side to side, answering her controls slowly; it was impossible to steer a decent compass course.

Within five minutes of changing course the engineer came forward and shouted in my ear that the inboard petrol pipe on the port engine was leaking badly. Then he climbed out on the wing and attempted to bind it with tape. The attempt was not successful.

I turned the nose of the boat for home. She started down wind at a rate of knots. In ten minutes we were eighteen miles on the homeward stretch. And the petrol pipe split from end to end. It was too bumpy to fly on one engine, so I shut both off and made a landing. The boat had a new design hull, and got into the heavy sea with ease. She rode light and free.

Three destroyers were slipping along at slow speed, about a mile away, rolling heavily in the beam sea. One of them turned out of line and headed for us. Her Commander flashed a signal asking if we wanted a tow. We did. The wind was blowing about thirty knots, and increasing!

The Commander crossed our bows, and a heaving-line snaked out. But with the wind and tide we were drifting very fast, and the line fell short. As the destroyer came around I put over a sea-anchor. This time the destroyer stopped across our bows. The heaving-line reached us. But we were in the lee, and our drift was checked. The destroyer, broadside on to the wind, came down on us before the sea-anchor could be cast adrift.

A wave threw us against the steel side. Once, twice, and with a crackling of mahogany the bow of the flying-boat was crushed in down to the waterline. One of the wings went on board the destroyer, and threatened to dump overboard the mines she was carrying on her stern. The crew of the destroyer, now all activity, fended us off with boat-hooks, hands, feet, and anything available. I cast off the sea-anchor. The destroyer went ahead. We drifted clear. The three other members of the crew were out on the tail keeping the bow out of the water.

I pulled in the heaving-line. To it was attached a grass line which I made fast to the towing pennant. We fitted a leather flying-coat over the hole in the bow. The destroyer went slowly ahead, and we followed after. The tow parted in an hour. Again the destroyer came alongside, again the bow was damaged, and again, after a time, the grass line parted.

It was now dark. A wire hawser was sent across, and we made it fast. The wire sank down in the water, and when the destroyer went ahead the bow of the flying-boat was pulled down. The flying-coat held for an instant, burst inwards, the sea rushed in, cascaded over the front bulkhead, and flooded the hull from bow to stern. The top of the boat was just above the surface of the water.

Luckily I was standing with the Very's pistol in my hand. I discharged it, and the destroyer stopped.

I reached down in the boat for the pigeons. Poor birds, they were drowned. The boat pitched forward suddenly, and the wireless operator and myself were thrown into the water. We climbed up again. But before I could do so I had to kick off a fine new pair of thigh-length flying-boots, woolly inside, which sank, and were lost.

A cutter was dropped from the destroyer to take us all off, and the Commander made a determined effort to salve the boat or the engines, but it ended in failure, the boat finally sinking.

This was the last patrol to be carried out in 1917.

In the eight and a half months of the life of the War Flight it had received fourteen flying-boats in all, five of which were still in good condition. With this small amount of material the pilots had carried out five hundred and fifty-four patrols, flown a distance of seventy-seven thousand and five hundred sea miles, brought a Zeppelin down in flames, sighted forty-four enemy submarines, and bombed twenty-five of them.

CHAPTER 6

Winged Huns and the Tale of the I.O.

ONE

Down in the Straits of Dover there was now in being a barrage which put the fear into the hearts of the crews of the German submarines.

All night long, across the narrow channel between the white chalk cliffs of Dover and Calais, a line of armed trawlers lit up the waves with brilliant flares, and prevented the U-boats from slipping through on the surface.

Beneath the water were nasty devices which, when encountered by an Under sea-boat trying to creep through submerged, brought its crew to a sticky end, and reduced the cunning mechanism of the submarine to scrap.

Between the coasts of England and France two cables were laid on the bottom, parallel to each other, and some distance apart. These cables had hydrophones on them at frequent intervals. A hydrophone is a water telephone. If a noise is made in the water, say by the twin propellers of a submarine revolving, the sound is picked up by the diaphragm in the hydrophone, which is similar to the diaphragm in a telephone, only, of course, bigger.

An enemy submarine going up or down through the Straits under water would cross one and then the other of these cables. His propeller noises would be picked up by the nearest hydrophones, and the listeners in the silent cabinets on the English coast could tell in which direction he was travelling, and his approximate position.

The skippers of the trawlers, those born hunters of Fritz, would be warned by wireless, and would hasten to the place and shoot a row of nets that is, lay them while under weigh across the path of the submarine. On these nets were hung mines, and the mines were connected to the trawlers by electric cables. The nets were made of wire, and had a large mesh, were very light, and each had a buoy which floated on the surface.

The Commander of a submarine running blind would barge into a net, drag it along, and the mines would be pulled in against the sides of his boat. The surface buoy would bob all the same as a fisherman's float. The skipper of the trawler, watchfully waiting, would press a heavy finger on the correct button.

The mother-ship in the German harbour would wait in vain for the return of her criminal son.

This was only one of the many methods of counter-fright fullness adopted, and so efficient were these Naval devilments that Fritz began to go north-about through the Fair Island Channel between the Orkneys and Shetlands, navigating south down the west coast of Scotland by sounding on the hundred fathom line, and the occupation of Felixstowe, so far as the intensive hunting of submarines was concerned, was gone.

But there were still a few Fritzes about, the Beef Trip had to be protected, and a demand arose for reconnaissance patrols in the Bight. Also the Hun had developed a fast monoplane fighter seaplane, with all its guns on the top line, and specially designed for fighting the flying-boats near the water.

These monoplanes, which were nasty fellows, carrying little fuel and fighting on their own front doorstep, were based on Zeebrugge in Belgium and the Island of Borkum in the Bight of Heligoland. In the fighting which now ensued the flying-boats, although designed for weight carrying and distance and not for fighting, held their own. A complete record of all encounters show honours even; besides which the flying-boats carried out their job o' work.

With the new year American pilots began to arrive for the War Flight. The first was Ensign Vorys, U.S.N., and Ensigns Fallen, Potter, Sturtevant, Hawkins, and Scheffelin quickly followed. They were splendid chaps, keen on flying, and could not be kept out of the air. They had all the fresh enthusiasm for the war which everybody that came in in 1914 and 1915 had possessed, and regarded patrolling, which the old hands looked on as a hard and exacting business, as a novel and entertaining sport. One of their number, who arrived a little later, looped the loop in a six-ton flying-boat; a feat which had not been performed before, and has not been tried since.

There was the deepest sorrow in the mess when Ensign Sturtevant and Ensign Potter were shot down. They were charming messmates, splendid pilots, and very gallant gentlemen.

The new year opened badly.

On the 2nd, in a thirty-knot wind, Gordon took off the harbour in a new type boat. As he rose from the water a petrol pipe failed, and not having height to turn he landed her outside down wind. She touched the water at a rate of knots, her bottom split open, and she sank in shallow water. Before she sank Gordon and his crew were taken off by a motor-boat.

The Old Man of the Sea organised a salvage party.

Jumbo boiled about in the sheds setting alight his trusty henchmen, and collected an amazing assortment of wire cables, ropes, balks of timber, flares, anchors, and what else I know not. The station tug *Grampus*, the steam hissing from her safety-valve through the zeal of her fireman (for the usual unexciting job of the crew was to bring bread and beef from Shotley, and this was an adventure), took the O.M.O.T.S.'s pet, the flat-bottomed salvage barge, in tow. They took it out and anchored it to windward of the wreck, but nothing further could be done until low water, which was at nine o'clock.

HUN MONOPLANE DIVING IN TO SHOVE HOME AN ATTACK

In the darkness of the night, in the shadow of the sheds, Jumbo collected his piratical crew and packed them into the Grampus. I asked to be taken along, and we all shoved out through the guard-ships into the open sea. We could not get near the barge owing to the shallow water, and Jumbo forsook us, climbing with five of his satellites into a small dingey, which, perilously overloaded, bobbed away over the heavy sea into the darkness.

A long wait. The tug was rolling and tossing in the steep waves. A drizzling rain was falling. There were no shore lights, and the night was pitch-black. And then there was a glare of light in the distance, Jumbo had lit one of the acetylene flares on the stern of the salvage barge. The glare increased, and presently a light came bobbing over the water towards the tug, it was a lantern in the bow of the dingey. I climbed across and was ferried to the scene of activity.

It was a weird sight.

Five hissing acetylene flares surrounded the wreck with a fierce glow. Intense darkness all around, and in the brilliant pool of light a section of tossing waves, the flying-boat with her lower wings showing on the surface of the water, and the oilskin-clad men working on her.

The wind was dying down, and as the tide fell the force of the waves was broken by the shoals over which they had already passed and by the barge. Jumbo took a short wire rope, with a wire hawser attached midway between the two ends, and had it worked down from the bow beneath the flying-boat. The ends were made fast to the engine bearer-struts, the men tying the knots under water, as the tide was now rising. Other men had made and fitted a wire sling for each engine, and to these two lines were made fast and taken to the barge, The slack in the wire hawser and the two lines was hauled in, and as the incoming tide raised the barge the flying-boat was lifted clear of the bottom.

As soon as the water was deep enough Jumbo had the anchor heaved up and two motor-boats took the barge in tow. The flying-boat, supported on the surface by its lower wings moving through the water, followed after. It was towed by the two lines attached to the engines, the wire bridle under the bow preventing it nose-diving.

The Old Man of the Sea processioned into the harbour in triumph. First the Grampus, then the two motor-boats, then the barge, and finally the flying-boat. He beached her at the Old Station at nearly high tide. A line was taken ashore and attached to a motor lorry. As the tide came in the boat was pulled farther and farther up the beach by the motor lorry, until it could be brought in no farther.

A gang of carpenters were turned out of their hammocks and placed shores under the wings to keep the boat on an even keel, and when the tide fell they patched the holes in the hull with three-ply wood and canvas.

At the next high tide the boat was floated off, towed to a slipway, put on a trolley and rolled up to a shed for repair. She was ready again in March, and carried out many more patrols.

During January 1918 there were only nine flying days, and although there were sixteen patrols carried out, no submarines were sighted.

About this time many disquieting rumours were circulating concerning the joining of the Royal Naval Air Service and the Royal Flying Corps into a new service disquieting because the seagoing men of the R.N.A.S. felt that they were nearer in spirit and work to the sailors than to the soldiers. Also the R.N.A.S. was a small show, the total personnel being about forty thousand, and it w r as felt that under new and unsympathetic management the work would suffer, work the value of which was just being recognised by a stern parent, the Navy.

Two

Fighting now commenced to be more or less common, the interference from the German fliers getting more intense as time went on.

The prime mover of the Huns seemed to be Commander

Christianson, a full-out merchant and apparently a sportsman, who was credited by the Felixstowe pilots with developing the fast little monoplane seaplane. He was stationed first at Zeebrugge, and when the harbour was wrecked by the Navy and mopped-up by the Army, after being thoroughly bombed by the Royal Naval Air Service, he went to Borkum.

He had been in the merchant service, but his wife had objected to his occupation as being too dangerous, and he had taken up seaplane flying before the war. He now led the pilots of the Marine Krestenflegen Abteilung Flandern, and he and his pilots were as hard as their name is to pronounce correctly.

The Germans did not develop flying-boats, because the work their pilots had to do was different from the work of the British pilots. One big four-engined boat was built, a horrid-looking monoplane, with fuselage sticking out behind, but it was crashed at Warnemünde on its trial flight, killing eight men.

The British wanted to bomb the submarines and carry out reconnaissance off the German coast the Germans wanted to stop them. Therefore the British built big machines for long distance and weight carrying, and the Huns built small handy machines for fighting. The boat type is most convenient for bomb-carrying and long reconnaissance; the float type for a light two-seated fighter.

The flying-boats, owing to their weight and two engines, were slow to manoeuvre. They were fitted with four gun positions, one in the bow and three in the tail. The gun mounting in the bow commanded almost all the forward hemisphere and a fair part of the rear over the top plane. But the three gun mountings in the boat behind the planes did not together have sufficient field of fire to protect the boat from an attack from the rear. In fact a boat did not have the fighting value of a machine with a single gunner who could fire in all directions that is, the value of a single-seated scout.

There are a good many yarns about the fighting.

There is the yarn of the three flying-boats looking for submarines out near the North Hinder.

The pilots were surprised by seven Huns who dived out of the clouds and sat upon their tails.

The leading boat was set on fire.

The pilot dived for the water. But before he got there his crew, seizing the fire-extinguishers which the boats always carried, put out the fire, and he climbed up again.

But the formation was broken and a dogfight commenced.

One boat was brought down, but on the way to the water the engineer shot down a monoplane in flames.

A second boat was brought down, but at the same time the combined fire of its guns crashed an enemy two-seater.

And then, as the enemy having had enough drew off, the third boat, its tanks and engines riddled with bullets, had to land.

So all three boats were down forty miles from shore.

The pilots of the first boat, the engines of which were completely disabled, were taken off by a destroyer and their boat taken in tow. The pilots of the other two boats plugged the bullet-holes in the bottoms and repaired their engines sufficiently well to taxi to England, where they arrived next morning.

There is also the story of the pilots who went out early one morning for an airing in an obsolete boat.

Five Huns met them off the Galloper Shoal and interrupted their promenade. They were shot down, crashed in the water, and turned bottom side up.

But all the crew got out safely and sat on the bottom of the boat. It was floating in a pool of pure petrol spilt out of its huge tanks, and the air was scarcely fit to breathe owing to petrol fumes. Said the wireless operator to the first pilot

"Sir, may I smoke? "

The crew were later rescued by two flying boats sent out to look for them.

But only the beginnings of the fighting are recorded, as most of the fighting took place after the 12th of April the date on which this yarn ends.

The first success in the fighting fell to Clayton and Adamson in *Old '61* on February 5.

They were out in the Spider Web with another boat looking for submarines when they found trouble. Five enemy seaplanes dived out of a cloud in formation and settled on their tail. The accompanying boat was some distance ahead, and the surprise was complete.

The engineer and wireless operator dived into the stern and got the rear guns in action. Clayton waggled the tail from side to side in order to give each man a clear field of fire alternately.

One of the enemy dived in to shove home an attack, and Robinson, the engineer, put a long burst from his machinegun into his engine. The Hun side-slipped, struck the water at speed, the floats collapsed, and the seaplane disintegrated into a twisted mass of wreckage.

The remaining four enemy seaplanes drew off, and the boats carried on.

But on February 15 the Huns got their own back.

Faux and Bailey in one boat, and Purdy and Sturtevant in another, were twenty-five miles past the old position of the North Hinder for this light-vessel, so familiar to the pilots at Felixstowe, had been removed by the Dutch authorities.

The pilots were some distance apart booming along looking for submarines, when seven winged Huns fell upon them. Purdy made a right-hand turn and steered in a south-westerly direction. Faux opened out his engines and started to turn after him; but his port engine failed, and he swung away to the left, thus opening the distance between himself and Purdy.

Faux found the air mixture control lever had moved forward with the throttle and had shut down one engine; but in the few seconds he took to put this right, three of the enemy were on top of him and four were on Purdy's tail.

Purdy was crashed in flames.

Faux now had five enemy seaplanes attacking him. He turned for England and roared over the sea, followed by the enemy. Each time they dived in they were met by a burst from the rear guns. Finally they kept well astern and sniped from long range. A bullet wrecked the two wind-driven petrol pumps, and the wireless operator had to leave one of the rear guns and pump up petrol by hand.

For thirty minutes the chase continued, and then Faux ran in to a bank of mist. When well in this he turned sharply to the right, the Huns overran him, lost him, and he returned safely to harbour.

This was the first boat shot down by the enemy, and there was sorrow in the Mess over the loss of the crew, both pilots being exceedingly fine fellows, and the ratings held in high esteem by their messmates.

Outside of the fighting February was a quiet month, there being only eleven flying days in all.

THREE

First the skirmish and then the fight.

March the 12th was a fine day, and three boats in formation were thirty miles off the Dutch coast. There was nothing in sight; the sea, the horizon, the sky, were clear. And then there were five Huns. It is as sudden as all that.

The enemy pilots, owing to the greater handability of their light-float seaplanes, could attack how and when they pleased. The pilots of the boats kept close formation in order to protect each other. The Huns attacked from the rear. The air was full of tracer-smoke. Such a heavy crossfire was developed from the stern guns that the enemy did not shove home an attack.

Twice the pilots of the flying-boats altered course, and twice the Huns tried to break the formation as they did so, for with the two alterations of course the boats were headed for England. The pilots of the boats had dropped their bombs in order to lighten themselves for manoeuvring in case they were separated.

As the eight machines roared over the sea the pilots of the boats saw a small enemy submarine directly ahead. It was a dirty brownish colour, with net-cutters at the bow and jumping cables from bow to stern. Four men were on the conning-tower.

When the boats passed over the U-boat the bow-gunners

fired at it, the stern-gunners were shooting at the Huns, and the Huns were shooting at the flying-boats. Near the Outer Gabbard buoy the enemy turned to the left and buzzed off.

Three more boats were run down the slipway.

One failed to get off, but the other two boomed out to look for the Hun.

Tiny and Fallon were in the leading boat, and Webster and Rhys Davis were in the second. It was a misty day.

Sixty miles out from land the pilots saw in front of them five little specks upon the water. As they came up with them they saw they were five Hun seaplanes waiting to attack our patrols, sitting on the water in order to conserve petrol.

Tiny and Webster drew close together until they were wing-tip to wing-tip. They dived at the hostile formation at a roaring hundred knots. The pilots of the five seaplanes started their engines, scuttered along the water, leaving five white streaks behind them, and took to the air in a good V formation.

But Tiny and Webster had the superior position: they were above and behind the enemy, and height to a flying-man is what the weather-gauge is to a seaman in a sailing-ship. They saw a ball of green fire shot out by the pilot of the leading Hun machine. At the signal each of the Huns turned sharply to the left and were in line ahead, flying at right angles to their previous course.

Sacrificing some of their height to increase their speed, the boat-pilots fell on the enemy line, their bow guns going. But now the Huns flew in a big circle, in order to protect each other's tails, with the two boat pilots in the centre.

But this formation was a mistake. For only the gunners in the two enemy two-seaters could each bring one gun to bear on the boats, while the gunners in each boat could bring a broadside of three guns to bear on the Huns.

Nicol, the wireless operator of *Old '61*, put a burst from his machinegun into one of the two-seaters. It remained on its course for a moment, the bow rose, and it zoomed into the air until it was vertically upright. At the top of its climb it seemed to hang for a moment stationary, the propeller futilely revolving. Then its tail slid into the water four hundred feet below. As it drove into the water tail first the wings were torn off and floated on the surface, but the fuselage containing the engine, and with the pilot and observer, kept right on and vanished.

Now the remaining four Huns dived for the water, got into line ahead, and started for the Belgian coast.

But this manoeuvre again left the flying-boats with the advantage of height, and they crashed down on the enemy, broke his line, the four Huns scattering in all directions. Tiny and Webster now picked out individual machines, separated, and went after them.

Webster was in *Old '61*. She was full of bullet-holes, and the front main spar on the lower port wing was shattered. But he drove down on top of a single-seater, his gunners got several bursts home, and the Hun side-slipped down into the water on one wing, making a reasonably good landing. The fight swept on leaving him behind.

Tiny attacked the second two-seater. A bullet from the gun of the Hun observer found a billet in the neck of the wireless operator, Grey. He collapsed in a welter of blood. The engineer, leaving his gun for a moment, seized the Red Cross outfit, broke the watertight box open with a kick, and administered first aid.

In the meantime Tiny passed immediately over the two-seater. The machines were so close that the bow gunner found himself face to face with the Hun observer. He saw him working furiously to clear a jam in his gun. He fired a burst, and the Hun collapsed over the side of the fuselage. The two-seater side-slipped and nose-dived towards the water, but the pilot regained control before he touched, and made off at right angles close to the water and one wing very much down.

Webster was on top of the two remaining Huns, who had now closed in to each other, and Tiny joined him. But the boat pilots could not close with the enemy to decisive range. All the remaining ammunition was passed forward to the front gunners, who sniped at long range, the Huns gradually opening out their lead.

When all their ammunition was expended, Tiny and Webster turned for home. The fight had lasted for thirty-eight minutes. Over a hundred bullet-holes were counted in *Old '61*.

Chief Steward Blaygrove announced dinner.

It had been a busy day, everybody was weary, and we began to file into the mess with a feeling of pleasure.

FOUR

The telephone bell rang.

Our new Intelligence Officer, a man of infinite energy, answered the call.

He had arrived the previous day, and as he had never been on a flying-boat station before, he examined everything with microscopic care. He installed a new system of operation orders, put in a new method for keeping records and signals, and arranged for the building of a new and spacious intelligence hut. He had gone to bed about midnight after confiding in me that after France he was going to have an easy time.

But on this morning he had been up at two o'clock and had been working furiously all day, without a chance of luncheon or tea. He now followed me into the mess and said

"There are four Hun destroyers off the North Hinder position; the S.N.O. wants three boats sent out."

Giving one hungry glance at the table, he hastened away to the intelligence hut to prepare the operation orders.

As the three flying-boats were rolled out on the slipway and their crews climbed on board, four lean destroyers glided down the harbour in line ahead and passed out between the guard-ships, bound on the same errand.

The three boats were shoved down the slipway, the pilots took to the air at eight o'clock and rapidly disappeared from our sight seaward in the gathering dusk. The boom of the engines tailed out and ceased. All was silence.

With the little group of pilots on the slipway I returned to the mess to finish my interrupted dinner.

But the I.O., who had not even had a plate of soup but was

very conscientious, was now encamped in the Flying Office, where he seemed to be sending a tremendous number of signals. He also had a long yarn with the Fire Commander in charge of the harbour searchlights and batteries, warning him to look out for the returning flying-boats.

Shortly after nine o'clock he received a telephone message from a coastguard stationed some ten miles up the coast, that one boat was returning. He joined me on the slipway and we stood together in the velvety darkness listening. But all we could hear was the tide gurgling around the piers beneath us. Presently we heard a faint *zoom-zoom* far in the distance, and then the unmistakable full-throated roar of the twin engines.

The pilot passed over us at six hundred feet, shedding red signal lights, but all that we could see of him were the four pointed flames standing back from the exhaust-pipes. There was to be a full moon, but it did not rise until later. The song of the engines ceased as the pilot shut them off and glided down. And then he was on the water and being towed into the slipway by a motor-boat.

Her crew came ashore and reported that they had been out to the position required and had seen nothing. The I.O. retired to the silence cabinet and got busy. He was carefully writing down and numbering each signal he sent or received in order to enter them in a big book he had started to keep.

A thick mist began to creep in from the sea. It swallowed up Harwich, the guard-ships, the destroyers at anchor, the trawlers lying on our landing water, the buoys, and the slipways.

At ten o'clock we heard the second boat returning. The Fire Commander switched on his searchlights to show up the water to the pilot, but the beams were diffused in the mist and the harbour was filled with a yellow luminous haze.

Through this haze we saw the flying-boat travelling at a tremendous pace. And we heard a loud smack. The pilot had hit the invisible water at speed. Up and up through the shining mist we saw thrown the black silhouette of the boat. It seemed to pause for an instant. We held our breath. Then the bow fell, and

THE BOAT THAT STOOD ON ITS NOSE

she nose-dived into the water with a sickening crash of breaking wood. She weighed six tons.

Immediately all the ships in the harbour added their searchlights to the glare. We saw the boat standing in an amazing fashion on her nose, her tail vertically upright, and resting on the leading edges of the wings.

Two motor-boats detached themselves from the slipway and raced to the wreck. Their crews found that the bow of the boat had broken off complete at the wings. The crew had been spilled out of her like peas out of a pod. The wireless operator and engineer were picked up uninjured, and then Faux, who had a slight scratch on his forehead. Finally they found Bill Bailey, the second pilot, paddling around in the water, his chart-board under one arm, unhurt, but very much distressed because he had dropped the weighted code-book, for the loss of which he would have to fill in innumerable forms.

Going out in a motor-boat I attached a rope to the tail of the wreck, pulled her over backwards, towed her in, and beached her at the Old Station. The harbour was again in darkness, all the searchlights had been switched off.

As this excitement died down a wireless signal was picked up from the third boat. It was incomplete, and said something about "gun flashes" and "Belgian coast." It was of course picked up by other wireless stations. It lit up the whole east and south coast. Signals poured in from the Harwich flotilla, the Dover patrol, Group Headquarters, the Admiralty, and the Air Ministry. Everybody in England seemed spoiling to get in on the fight. The I.O. stood at the telephone taking down signals, until the silence cabinet looked as though it had contained a snowstorm.

I panicked over to the wireless hut. Here, in the soundproof cabinet, behind the double glass door, sat two operators, receivers clipped on their ears, listening intently. One of them closed a switch, a motor behind me buzzed, there was a series of sharp cracks, and the room was lit up by a steely electric glare. It was the spark jumping across the rotary gap, one of the operators had crashed a wireless signal out into the night. The buzz of the motor ceased. I looked through the glass doors the two operators, with intent faces, were again listening.

Spring-heeled Jack opened the door, said a word to the operators, and then went to the telephone. He was put through to the harassed I.O., and said

"I am sending out the call sign of the boat every five minutes, but so far she has not answered, and I cannot make anything more out of her first signal than I gave you. It was very faint, and there was a good deal of interference."

I went back to the flying office.

At eleven o'clock the I.O. received a hostile aircraft warning. All lights on the station were extinguished, and the hands turned out to stand by their dugouts, which had been constructed after the Gothas had raided the station twice in daylight. The I.O. seemed glued to the telephone taking in signals. The first one ran

"Hostile aircraft attacking lightship in Thames estuary."

And then they came in fast. The I.O. was working by the light of an electric torch. These signals said that ships all over the estuary were reporting enemy aircraft, that some of the coast batteries were in action, that more batteries were in action, that the first warning was out in the Metropolitan police area, that night-flying machines were up from a dozen aerodromes, and finally, that the "take cover" warning was out in London.

I went out into the mist on the slipway. I heard the thudding of guns, and saw star-shells bursting high in the air in the direction of the mouth of the Thames. Nothing had been heard of the third boat, and I was very much worried. The I.O. back at the telephone was still fighting with a blizzard of signals.

About one o'clock things quieted down, and the all-clear signal came in. The I.O. told me he was going up to the mess for a much-needed cup of cocoa. But as he was about to put his hand on the knob of the flying office door the telephone bell rang, and his work began again. Another air raid warning came in, battery after battery was reported in action, and London again took to the cellars. The fuss continued until nearly two o'clock, when another all-clear signal came in. The I.O. was looking a bit pinched about the face, and white under the gills.

I again went out on the slipway and listened for the missing boat, and was joined by the I.O. Presently, in the distance, we heard the faint note of a twin-engined machine. It developed into the roar of a pair of Rolls, which passed over us in the mist. We fired Very's lights from the end of the slipway, and the Fire Commander switched on two searchlights to light up the guard-ship at the boom. Suddenly the roar of the engines ceased, and all was silent. We heard nothing more.

Shoving off one motor-boat to search the harbour, I sent a second outside, and followed it in a third, with a good stock of Very's lights. After barging around in the mist for half an hour, shedding a copious display of red, white, and green fireballs, I fell in with the missing boat, passed the pilots a line, and towed them in. The pilots, MacLauren and Dickey, reported to the I.O., and we went up to the mess for sandwiches and cocoa.

We left a weary I.O. at the telephone trying to straighten out the tangled skein of events.

MacLauren, as soon as he left the harbour, lost sight of the other two boats in the gathering dusk. Just outside the harbour, and before they had got out through the minefields, he overhauled our four destroyers which had got away before him. Looking down, he saw them all in a lather over doing thirty knots. He left them behind as though they were nailed to the water.

When he made the North Hinder position he flew around in great circles but came across no Hun destroyers. It was a fine night for flying, not a bump in the air, so he turned south-west. In half an hour he saw a light winking ahead on the water and picked up the Schouen Bank buoy.

Here he turned south down the Belgian coast and soon saw gun-flashes in the distance. It was the never-ceasing artillery duel on the Flanders front. But his optimistic wireless operator thought it was a naval action in full swing, and got off part of a wireless signal before he could be stopped. When a wash-out signal was being sent the transmitter broke down.

But during the discussion MacLauren had got over Zeebrugge, and the boat was surrounded by flaming onions. The whole misty atmosphere was filled with a green glare. Dickey dived into the front cockpit to drop the bombs, but before doing so looked back at the pilot.

MacLauren saw the smile wiped off Dickey's face, his jaw drop, and his frantic signal to turn out to sea.

Not knowing what horror had shattered the composure of the usually imperturbable Dickey, MacLauren banked the heavy boat round in a split-all turn and drove out over the water. As he did so he looked back over his shoulder to see the terror behind, but all he saw was the placid face of the full moon, just risen, and looking very red through the mist.

Dickey in the front cockpit, intent on dropping the bombs, had turned suddenly and got a partial glimpse of its red face through the engine bearer-struts. He thought it was some new and awful devilment of the Hun, and automatically made the signal to turn out to sea.

MacLauren now headed for home. The mist was thick and the farther he flew the thicker it got. While skimming close over the surface of the water he found a lightship and circled around it. The wireless operator took his Aldis lamp and flashed to the crew, asking for the position. But he received no answer.

So MacLauren barged around in the Thames estuary, happening upon a good deal of shipping, and finally found himself over the coast. Here big guns began to go off. Star-shells and high explosives were bursting at about fourteen thousand feet. He was only up about six hundred, kiteing along in the mist, the concussions from the discharge of the guns shaking the boat. He fled up along the coast over battery after battery. Then he turned out to sea.

Dickey wrote on a pad: "There must be the devil of a big air raid on." And MacLauren nodded.

When things got more or less quiet MacLauren ventured in again, saw a place which looked like Harwich harbour, and landed. But it wasn't. However, he shut off the engines. Then he heard night-flying machines passing overhead, and knowing that if he met up with any of the eager young pilots bent on bloodshed they would shoot first and inquire afterwards, he lay snug on the water. The sandwiches and the thermos flask were got out and the chart was carefully examined.

As soon as the hick-boo was over MacLauren had the engines started and took off. Once in the air he saw that the batteries had started up again. But he now knew where he was and flew straight up the coast to Felixstowe, landing outside, as he did not want to knock over a ship or two in the mist.

It was now four o'clock.

As we were rising from the table to go to our cabins the door of the mess opened. There stood the I.O. drooping with fatigue, but with a neatly filed and indexed bundle of signals six inches thick in his hand. He went up to MacLauren and said——

"There were no Gothas. Do you realise, young man, that this night you have put everybody in London into their cellars twice?"

At early breakfast next morning the I.O. received an urgent order from the Powers That Be to report elsewhere immediately for important duties, and an hour later as he was departing he said to me——

"I am sorry to go. I had no idea that a flying-boat station was such a busy place."

Chapter 7

Into the Bight and End of L 53

One

With lustful pride the Huns called the North Sea the German Ocean, and if there was any part of this dirty sheet of water which justified the name, it was that portion known as the Bight of Heligoland.

Here before the war were the growing harbours and ship-yards with which she was challenging the British supremacy of the sea; and during the war her yards which turned out submarines, her seaplane and Zeppelin bases, and the refuges of her High Seas Fleet.

Climbing into a flying-boat and crossing a hundred miles of sea, brings you to the Hook of Holland. Turning north you pass Scheveningen, which is near The Hague, where peace conferences met to mitigate the horrors of war, or do away with it entirely, and supplied the Hun with a ready-made list of forbidden atrocities—atrocities which he immediately made haste to perpetrate.

Passing up the coast you come to the Dutch islands of Texel, Vlieland, Terschelling, and Ameland. Once around the corner of Terschelling Island, and you are in the Bight.

If you draw a line true north-east from this island it will touch Denmark just below the Horn Reefs, near the boundary-line between Schlesvig and Jutland, and all the water to the east of this line is the Bight, the particular property, more or less, during the war, of the Hun seaplanes, the Zeppelins, and the German Navy.

Going along the coast from Terschelling into the Bight you find the island of Borkum, in the mouth of the Ems river. The Hun seaplane pilots stationed here carried out reconnaissance and bombing patrols out to the Dogger Banks and down to the Dutch coast. A short distance up the Ems is Emden, one of the bases from which the pirate Fritz sallied forth to do his dirty work.

Continuing, you pass the island of Norderney with its sea-plane station, and reach the Jade river, with Wilhelmshaven, an important seaplane and submarine base. In the angle of the coast are the Zeppelin sheds of Wittmundshaven. Farther on is the Weser river, with Vagesack and Bremen, which spawned out the Undersea-boats, and the Zeppelin base of Ahlhorn.

Turning north you find the Zeppelin sheds of Nordholz, and reach Cuxhaven, the place made famous by the celebrated raid of the R.N.A.S. early in the war. Here in the Elbe is Brunsbut-tel, a submarine base, on the North Sea end of the Kiel Canal, and farther up the river is Hamburg, where once upon a time German shipowners dreamed dreams of possessing the maritime supremacy of the world.

Some thirty miles outside the coast, and protecting the mouth of the Elbe, you come across the fortified island of Heligoland, with its fine artificial harbour for war vessels, its submarine base, and its seaplane station. The guns of Heligoland were of great range, and threw a tremendous weight of metal, and could prevent our surface ships from approaching within a radius of twenty miles.

I was informed by a Royal Naval Air Service officer, who had a good deal to do with the successful attack on Zeebrugge and Ostend, that he had a plan to destroy the garrison of Heligoland by means of poison gas and an attack under smokescreens, but that those in authority considered the scheme too barbarous, as everybody on the island would have perished.

Going north from Heligoland you come to Sylt Island, with its seaplane base, and inside on the mainland the Zeppelin sheds of Tondern, destroyed by naval aeroplanes flown from the deck of H. M.S. *Furious*. Just north of Sylt you pass out of the Bight near the Horn Reefs.

So the Bight was the hotbed of all German naval schemes, and they ploughed it with the keels of their ships, and sowed it with mines, and the British Navy could not follow the Hun fleet inside or prevent their submarines coming out. The British Navy, as soon as they could collect sufficient mines, and there was a great shortage of mines in the first years of the war, mined the Germans in their turn, until the Hun surface ships and submarines had finally to make their way out behind a row of minesweepers.

Flying-boat pilots from England could get into the Bight, but it was a long way away, and they could not get in far enough or stay long enough to do very useful work. So Colonel Porte, at Felixstowe, devised the towing-lighters. These lighters were little flat-bottomed steel barges, with hydroplane bottoms, on which the flying-boats could crawl up. They could be towed, with the boats in place, by a destroyer at thirty knots.

The idea was to put flying-boats on the lighters, tow them across to the Bight behind destroyers, and slip them into the water. The boats, not having first to cross the North Sea, would have enough petrol to carry out long reconnaissance and return to England.

Early in 1918 the Navy was preparing the pleasant little surprise for the Huns at Zeebrugge and Ostend. While the assault was in progress it was essential that the ships engaged in the attack should not be fallen upon by the enemy from the rear. Therefore their north flank was to be protected by the Harwich Light Forces cruising off Holland.

But besides this, the Navy people wanted to know what

chance there was of the German Fleet coming out. Under ordinary circumstances the Huns would have to go a long way round, because of our minefields; but they might have got wind of the show, and be sweeping a shortcut passage through them, to be used by a strong striking force.

Our surface ships could not of course go in for the information, the submarines had done all that they could, airships were out of the question because of Hun seaplanes, so the flying-boats were told to do the job.

Thus it came about that the first two lighter trips were carried out in the Bight.

Two

At noon on March 2 we were ordered to prepare to go into the Bight.

I chose the three best machines out of the War Flight string of nine boats, and the men groomed them to a finish.

Everything that was put on board was carefully weighed and the total weight checked to a nicety, so as to make certain that the pilots could get off in the open sea.

Norman A. Magor, a Canadian from Montreal, was chosen to lead the flight. He was a fine pilot. He had taken a boat from Felixstowe to Dunkirk, when the float seaplane pilots there had packed up because of the deadliness of the Hun fliers. While there he destroyed the German submarine U-C 72 just off Zeebrugge. Later on while on patrol from Felixstowe, in a fight against overwhelming odds, his boat was shot down in flames. He was a gallant gentleman.

In the evening, as the light was fading, the three boats were rolled out on the concrete, an electric heater, to keep the oil warm, was clipped on beneath each engine, and thick padded covers fitted, to keep the heat in, so that the engines would start easily. They were shoved down the slipway and turned over to the Old Man of the Sea.

Jumbo was in his element. His motor-boats seized the flying-boats as they touched the water and towed them to the

LIGHTER WITH FLYING – BOAT BEING TOWED IN HEAVY SEA

sterns of their appointed lighters, which were lying at buoys at the ends of the slipways. The five men in the crew of each lighter had flooded the water-tanks in the sterns, and the boats were quickly floated into their cradles, hauled up by a winch into position and secured. With a hiss the compressed air was turned into the tanks, the water was blown out, and the lighters rose into towing trim.

Now the pilots carrying their flying gear assembled on the slipway. I checked the crews over and asked if everybody was ready. On this a great cry arose from Jumbo he had forgotten his provisions, and in answer to the cry we saw men staggering down the concrete under the weight of huge boxes. The Old Man of the Sea never went on an expedition without a good supply of food.

We were ready.

The night was still, not a breath of air was stirring, and a light haze hung over the oily-smooth surface of the harbour.

Heralded by the mournful wail of a siren three destroyers loomed up beside the lighters. They had slipped across the harbour without their sharp sheerwaters raising a ripple. Jumbo leaped into activity. The noisy exhausts of three motor-boats shattered the silence, we all found ourselves bumped on board, and in two minutes the lighters were off their buoys and at the sterns of their respective destroyers.

I was going out in the leading destroyer to watch the evolution, and Jumbo was going out on the leading lighter.

As we fetched up at our destroyer she switched on a yardarm group, lighting up the flying-boat and her own stern with the waiting men. Jumbo sprang on board the lighter and received the wire hawser, making it fast to the towing bollards. A waterproof electric cable was passed to carry the current for the electric heaters.

The lighter, swinging with the tide, tried to put one of the wings of the flying-boat on board the destroyer, but the wing was successfully fended off by an active bluejacket, with a pudding-bag on the end of a boat-hook, a weapon which had been prepared for just such an emergency. The pudding-bag was a piece of cloth stuffed with soft odds and ends, fastened to the business end of the boat-hook to prevent any injury to the planes.

In the meantime the motor-boat ran alongside the destroyer with the flying crew, and we climbed on board. As we landed on the deck her siren gave a short blast, the yardarm group was extinguished, and she went ahead. I looked astern and could just see the other two destroyers with their lighters following. From the time of leaving the slipway five minutes had not elapsed.

As we passed out between the guard-ships into the expectant darkness of the North Sea the tow was lengthened, and I went up on the bridge.

Behind us on the lighter were Jumbo and his four men, settling down for the night in the cramped forecastle, in which were two bunks, an electric heater tapped off the main cable, and a big box of provisions.

Once outside our minefields we were picked up by the covering force of light cruisers and destroyers, and we started across for the Texel at eighteen knots. Fascinated by the brooding mystery of the darkness and the rush through the black water at a pace which seemed greater than the speed of a flying-boat, I spent most of the night on the bridge, being comforted at intervals with cocoa, excellent cocoa which can only be had on board ship. But before daybreak I snatched two hours' sleep in Number One's bunk.

I had apparently just closed my eyes when I was turned out by a message that I was wanted on the bridge. As I climbed the iron ladder the unearthly light of the false dawn was filtering through the darkness. Far away on the port bow I saw the light cruisers, grey ships barely discernible on a grey sea.

A signal had come through to stand by.

There was a round wind of ten knots blowing, ruffling the surface of the water. It promised to be a fine morning for flying.

We came upon some fishing smacks and then the Haaks lightship, black and gaunt against the light in the east, and strange and unfamiliar when seen for the first time from the level of the water. Here the whole flotilla turned south for ten miles, and at six o'clock the signal for zero time was received.

Jumbo, on the lighter, had the covers stripped from the engines and the heaters removed. At the same time the tow was shortened and Magor and Potter and the two ratings were transferred. They started the engines of the flying-boat, tested them full out, and then throttled them down until they were just ticking over. Webster and Fallon in the second boat, and Clayton and Barker in the third boat, had also tested their engines.

When the correct time had elapsed the engines of the flying-boats were stopped, the destroyers slowed down to three knots, and the boats were slid off the lighters backwards into the water. The destroyers made a right-hand turn and drew away from them.

The warships formed a four-mile circle, travelling at speed in case an Undersea-boat was lurking about. In the centre, bobbing up and down on the water, were the three boats, looking incredibly small. Presently I saw white water breaking beneath their bows, they ran along the water, bucketing a bit in the swells created by the ships, and took to the air.

Getting into formation they headed in a north-easterly direction and gradually diminished in size until they were no more than specks in the sky.

Then I lost sight of them.

When he had got off Terschelling, Magor swung his formation east and went into the Bight. They photographed all minesweepers and surface craft they met and jotted their position on the chart. At Borkum they ran into two two-seater Hun seaplanes.

Magor crashed down on the tail of the first seaplane and Potter filled it with lead from his machinegun. It burst into flames, nose-dived into the water, and a pennant of black smoke, ever increasing in volume, tailed off down wind.

Clayton fell upon the second seaplane, his gunner failed to get a burst home, and the fleeing Hun was chased to Borkum, where he landed behind the island close to a gunboat.

But the Hun observer in the seaplane Magor brought down had riddled the flying-boat with bullets. Great gashes were torn in the petrol tanks, fortunately above the level of the liquid, and a water-pipe on the port engine was pierced.

Magor shut down that engine and flew on the other.

The other two boats joined him and the formation proceeded on the appointed courses, taking photographs and making notes.

In the meantime Anderson, Magor's engineer, stripped off his leather flying-coat and climbed out on the wing to the damaged engine. He was passing through the air at sixty knots. It whipped his clothing against his arms and legs, making them difficult to move; it tried to wrench his tools and materials from his hands, and would have blown him overboard had he relaxed his vigilance. For one hour, an hour completely filled with sixty long minutes, he fought with the air and completed the repair.

Magor, when he could start up his second engine, was two hundred miles from Felixstowe, and had completed his reconnaissance, so he turned the formation for home, crossed the North Sea, and landed in the harbour at half-past twelve o'clock.

Nineteen days later the second lighter trip was sent into the Bight.

Tiny Galpin and Rhys Davis were leading, Webster and Tees were in the second boat, and Barker and Galvayne were in the third. The latter pilot was killed later when the pilots of four boats attacked fifteen Huns off Terschelling, and put them to flight.

Tiny led his flight into the Bight, and also encountered two enemy seaplanes. But these pilots were not having any. They dropped their bombs and made off inland at high speed.

He met a flotilla of minesweepers who fired shells at him. So he and the other two pilots swooped down and swept the decks with machinegun fire. When the minesweeper first opened fire the wireless operator seized his Aldis lamp and began signalling furiously to one of the ships. Tiny, reaching out, pulled him away from the side and demanded an explanation. The operator wrote on his pad——

"Sir, he was making e's to me."

He had not realised they were enemy craft, and thought that the quick flash of the gun was the light of a signal-lamp with which somebody was making a series of *e*'s to him, the calling-up signal.

After sweeping around in the Bight as requisite, Tiny headed his formation for home. But now Webster's engines developed trouble, and he had to land three times to make repairs before the coast of England was sighted.

As a result of these two reconnaissances it was decided that the Huns were not making any serious effort to sweep a short-cut channel through our minefields, so they were not aware of the show to be staged at Zeebrugge and Ostend. The pilots engaged in the operation received a letter of appreciation from the Lords of the Admiralty.

THREE

Illustrating the work of the lighters, although the incident did not take place until late in 1918, there is the yarn about Zeppelin L 53.

Many subsequent lighter trips were attended by this Zeppelin. Its crew watched the evolution from a great height. The pilots of the flying-boats when slipped from their lighters were unable to get at the airship, as they were heavily laden with petrol. Her skipper, Commander Proells, kept well out of range of the anti-aircraft guns of the cruisers, and he thought himself safe enough.

But the L 53 annoyed Colonel Samson, D.S.O., who at this time was Officer Commanding No. 4 Group, R.A.F., and he had a thirty-foot deck made to fit on one of the towing lighters, and on this, held in place with a quick release gear, he put a Camel aeroplane, a single-seated fighter land-machine with great speed and climb.

On the first experiment, and while being towed by a destroyer at thirty knots, Colonel Samson tried to take the Camel off the lighter. But the deck was not at the right angle and the machine stalled off, nose-dived into the water, the lighter passing over the pilot and aeroplane. Both were fished out. Undeterred by this mishap he had the deck altered, and on the second trial it proved satisfactory, the aeroplane getting away in good style.

It was decided to have a go at the Zeppelin on the next lighter trip, and Cully, a Canadian, one of the old R.N.A.S. pilots, was chosen for the job and was told to stand by.

On August 11 a little show was to be staged in the Bight.

The Harwich light cruisers were to carry six coastal motor-boats to a position off Terschelling Island. Here they would be dropped into the water and sent well into the Bight over the minefields to torpedo any minesweepers and other surface craft, and collect if possible information which would make glad the heart of the Admiralty Intelligence Department.

About this department an American who had occasion to deal with them said——

"That gang is one that delivers the goods every time. I don't believe the boys in the U.S.A. can teach them anything. They look outside like an out-of-date, low-pressure, single-cylinder show, but inside, believe me, customer, they're a nickel-plated, triple-expansion, consume-their-own-smoke outfit, working above the licensed pressure and with a nigger on the safety-valve."

The show was to be all the same as putting in ferrets. The coastal motor-boats were small hydroplanes filled full of big engines and could do forty knots full out. They carried a torpedo on their stern and a machinegun mounted in the cockpit. Three flying-boats on lighters were to accompany the cruisers. They were to get off and keep in touch with the C.M.B.'s to direct them to enemy craft and lead them safely back to the ships, as owing to their liveliness on a rough sea their compasses were not of much value. The Camel was to go along on the lighter as a surprise packet for Old Man Zeppelin. Three more flying-boats were to leave Yarmouth and pick up the cruisers at Terschelling.

At daybreak on the morning appointed the whole circus was on the job.

At six o'clock the towing hawsers of the lighters were shortened and the crews of the flying-boats and Cully were put on board their respective machines. The three flying-boats were slipped, but their pilots could not get them off the water owing to a long swell, the absence of wind, and a heavy overload of petrol and armament. They were taken up on the lighters again.

But the light cruisers dropped the C.M.B.'s. They immediately dug out towards the Bight at top speed, flinging the tops of the rollers into spray far on each side of them, so that it looked as though they were supported on white and gleaming wings.

The three flying-boats from Yarmouth boomed up, and on receiving the order started on after the C.M.B.'s.

The flotilla then cruised off Terschelling until fifteen minutes after eight o'clock, when the flagship signalled to the destroyer towing the Camel lighter that the L 53 had been sighted.

Immediately Cully saw the Zeppelin glistening in the sunlight.

It was about thirty miles away, at a height of ten thousand feet.

It looked about as big as his little finger.

He climbed into the cockpit of his machine. The propeller was swung. He tested the rotary engine.

When the towing destroyer had got up to thirty knots, he ran his engine full out, slipped the quick release, ran along the lighter deck only five feet, and took to the air.

At forty-one minutes after eight o'clock he started to climb towards Commander Proells' airship at a speed of fifty-two miles an hour.

In the meantime the crews of the Yarmouth flying-boats had sighted the Zeppelin. Owing to some misunderstanding they returned to the light cruisers to report, and received an order to return to their base.

When the flying-boats were just out of sight on the homeward journey, fifteen Hun monoplanes appeared in the sky. They had been summoned from Borkum by the Zeppelin with wireless. They swept over the flotilla, dropping bombs on the ships, which replied by filling the surrounding atmosphere with bursting shells. It was a lively five minutes. With all the bombs that were dropped no hit was registered on a ship, but a shell found a monoplane and brought it down. At this, and having unloaded all their bombs, the fourteen Huns withdrew.

On their way back to Borkum the monoplanes met the C.M.B.'s. The motor-boats separated and ran along at forty knots, twisting, turning, doubling. But the Huns were all over them, firing into the thin shells of the structures streams of machinegun bullets. The crews of the boats replied with their machineguns. But it was a fight against heavy odds.

The engine of one boat was knocked out by a bullet. It stopped. The Hun monoplanes swooped down like gulls on a fish. The pilots tore the boat to pieces with bullets and it began to sink. But another C.M.B. hurled itself alongside and took off all the crew, wounded and unwounded.

Three C.M.B.'s in all were sunk, their crews being taken off under the greatest difficulties and dangers by the crews of the three surviving boats, and after a long contest the crews of these boats won their way to Holland, where they were interned.

During this time Cully in the Camel had been climbing steadily, all unaware of the fighting going on below him. He climbed the first thirteen thousand feet in twenty minutes. He had edged in towards the Dutch coast and was now between the coast and the Zeppelin and hidden from her crew by the sun.

Commander Proells had also been climbing, and he was still above Cully. His airship was of the type known as the height-climbing 50's, the last word in construction, six hundred and forty feet long, with five engines, and containing two million cubic feet of inflammable gas.

The L 53 had all this time been broadside on to Cully. He now saw her turn end on. He thought that he had been sighted by her crew, and that her Commander had turned out to sea away from him. He swung the nose of the Camel directly towards her and continued to climb. But he saw that the great airship was growing bigger and bigger. He realised at last that she was heading straight for him.

The two aircraft were closing with tremendous rapidity.

Cully was at eighteen thousand feet.

Commander Proells was at nineteen thousand feet.

He felt the controls of the Camel get sloppy and knew he could get it to climb no higher.

If Commander Proells could get up another couple of hundred feet he could not attack him with any chance of success.

But the crew of the great Zeppelin apparently did not see the tiny midge in the sun, for they held on their course at the same height.

At forty-one minutes after nine o'clock, one hour after Cully had left the lighter in the Camel, the two machines met head on, the airship only two hundred feet above the aeroplane.

Cully pulled back his controls and stalled his machine until the Camel was almost standing on its tail.

As the bow of the Zeppelin came into his sight he started both Lewis guns. The port gun jammed after fifteen rounds. But the other gun ran through its tray of ninety-seven rounds.

Cully looking through his telescopic sight, saw the flaming incendiary bullets darting into the dark belly of the airship.

He also saw a side of one of the four gondolas, a propeller flapping slowly around, and was three-quarters of the way down the body of the airship when his second gun stopped owing to the lack of ammunition.

So intent was he on the job that he did not know whether he was being fired at or not, but rather thought he was not.

With the stopping of his second gun he dived away to the right, looking back over his shoulder. The Zeppelin was going strong. It appeared to be undamaged. He had failed.

And then he saw three little bursts of flames.

They were on the envelope about sixty feet apart, and as he watched the flames increased in size with terrible rapidity.

Satisfied, he turned back to his instruments and got the Camel, which had been panicking all over the shop, in hand.

When he looked again L 53 was slowly falling,, burning furiously at the bow.

The nose bent down and broke off.

A black bundle in flames shot past him. It was one of the

crew who had jumped out of a gondola. He had a parachute and was the only survivor, being picked up by a Dutch vessel.

The aluminium skeleton of the bow of the Zeppelin was now fully exposed. But the fabric of the tail was still smoking and burning. She was standing vertically upright, nose down, and was falling rapidly below him with ever-increasing momentum.

Then he could see her no more because of the smoke.

As L 53 fell she left behind her a column of light blue smoke. He noticed that it was blown into the shape of a huge question mark.

Having finished the Zeppelin, Cully suddenly awoke to the need of looking out for himself. He flew straight to the Dutch coast, went south until he arrived at the Texel, and then went out to the rendezvous at Terschelling Bank. Here, at six thousand feet, there were patchy clouds between him and the water, and he could see no destroyers.

His pressure petrol tank ran out.

He switched over to the emergency gravity tank. It contained only enough petrol for twenty minutes, not nearly enough for him to get back safely to the Dutch coast.

Looking down, he saw a providential Dutch fishing boat, and decided to land beside it. As he dived down he saw two destroyers come out from under the edge of a cloud. And then he saw the whole flotilla. Looping and rolling over the fleet to relieve his pent-up feelings, he picked up his destroyer with the lighter, fired a light as a signal, and landed in front of her. He was picked up, the Camel was hoisted on the lighter, and the flotilla started back for Harwich.

FOUR

Here end the yarns about the beginnings and first year of the War Flight. On the 12th of April I began to turn over the little show to my successor, and took up work under the Technical Department, a shore job.

The high lights in the picture alone have been painted in, the grilling hours of monotonous and apparently unproductive patrol put in by the pilots over that grim and unfriendly graveyard of ships, the North Sea, have been left out. Results only have been more or less fully presented, the loyal and often heartbreaking work of the ratings in the sheds has not even been sketched. But the hard and the soft, the comedy and the tragedy, are now in the past, and it is out of such stuff, seemingly raw and grey at the time, that Romance is made.

****

The German submarines, defeated and surrendered, have come streaming in through the guard-ships, up past the slipways, their crews on deck, and the white ensign flying above them, and are lying rusting and rotting, huddled together, in "Submarine Trot" off Parkeston, in Harwich harbour.

New and better flying-boats than we used have been built. And *Old '61*, her day done, has been dismantled and broken up. But glance down the bare bones of her career.

1917	March	Launched
	April	First patrol on Spider Web
		First enemy submarine sighted
		Bombed submarine
		Sighted submarine
		Sighted submarine
		Bombed submarine
		Encountered four enemy destroyers
	May	Submarine bombed by consort
	June	Met six winged Huns
	October	Carried out first lighter trials
	December	Exchanged shots with four Huns
1918	January	Hull worn out, new one fitted
	February	Met eight Huns off Zeebrugge
		Engaged five Huns, one shot down
	March	Engaged five Huns, two shot down
		First lighter trip into Bight
	April	Handed over for experimental work
	October	Dismantled

Hours of patrol work   300
Total flying time   368

Also the men of the War Flight are mostly back in civilian life.

CULLY'S CAMEL ON WAY TO TERSCHELLING

They were nearly all 1914 and 1915 men, competent "tradesmen," cheerfully working overtime at their trades for a small wage, while men outside, absolutely free from discipline, were making big money for similar work. Not that the men were working for the money in it. They worked to down the Hun. But the point is mentioned because the high cost of living hit many of these service men very hard.

The officers are now scattered to the four corners of the earth, such as are still alive, in South Africa, Ceylon, Canada, South America, and the United States. There are few of them remaining in the new service. As required by the nature of the work, they were nearly all a bit older than the usual run of aeroplane pilots, and a peace time service made no appeal.

For "them as likes figures" the work they did in twelve months may be boiled down to——

April 13, 1917 to April 12, 1918

8	average number of boats a month
190	flying days
605	patrols carried out
105,397	nautical miles flown
47	enemy submarines sighted
25	enemy submarines bombed
1	Zeppelin destroyed

Also, at this time, the Service we belonged to and loved came to an untimely end, and although the War Flight carried on until the Armistice, and did great work under the Royal Air Force, the rose by another name did not smell as sweet.

****

On the last day of March there was a dinner given by the Mess to Rear-Admiral Cayley, C.B. He was a staunch friend of the Station, and had been in charge of operations from Harwich. But even he was leaving to take up new duties.

At this dinner many admirable speeches were made, both in style and substance, encouraging the Royal Naval Air Service pilots to play the game, and wholeheartedly turn over their allegiance to the new service that was being born at midnight a service which many of the active service men felt might open the door for intrigue and unrest, and quick and unfortunate changes in command and policy, at a time when all hands should be busy mopping up the Hun.

But the Royal Naval Air Service was passing away.

It was the older of the two British flying services, having its beginnings in 1910. It had never been noted for its red-tape methods, its ingenuity in creating forms to be filled in, or the number of ground personnel required to administer it. But the debt which the nation owes to it for the development of engines and efficient aircraft, no less than for its operations on land and sea over the whole world, has hardly been appreciated. For at one time, without the pilots developed under its traditions and the machines and engines developed by its foresight, things would have gone hard with our arms in France.

It was a small service that had done great things. But its work was not appreciated, as it followed the traditions of its parent, and adopted, not without a struggle it is true, the virtue of silence. And now its people were asked to give up the legends about the mighty pilots who had created the service, the traditions which had accumulated so rapidly in war time, the uniform and routine which so well fitted their work, the comradeship which had permeated the personnel owing to its limited number, and the name which numberless brave men had laid down their lives to make honourable.

And bitterest pill of all, the Navy, our natural parent, was willing we should be put under the guardianship of an unknown and alien stepmother.

****

At this dinner the toast to the King was drunk in the mess sitting for the last time.

****

Blow this khaki! I feel hardly human.

CHAPTER 8

The Future: Running the U.S. Mail

Lotus-eating down among the South Sea Islands, knocking about in a little old topsail schooner, trading a bit for occupation and not for profit, yet getting out with a pleasant balance on the right side, I had drowsily drifted down the river of life ten years nearer to the Great Uncharted Sea.

When I sloughed off my uniform at the end of the Great War, worn out in body, weary in mind, and sick with the so-called civilisation which had produced such a Frankenstein monster, I had promised myself a two-year holiday far from cities, telephones, and newspapers, and the two years had quietly and unobtrusively grown into ten.

Now, having travelled nearly around the world by devious and dawdling routes, and that morning having sauntered down the gangplank of a rusty and battered old tramp steamer, I was standing in a street in Plymouth, rather dazed and bewildered by the noise and crowd of the busy seaport town.

Without a moment's warning, with an appalling suddenness, I staggered beneath a tremendous blow between my shoulder-blades, and a voice roared in my ear "Pix, by all that's holy!"

Half turning, I saw a short stocky man, in a blue uniform,

who was now trying to dislocate the bones in my right hand, and more or less succeeding.

"You don't know me," he shouted, laughing. "But you're the same old, thin, dried-up specimen you always were. I'd have known you anywhere. I'm Pank."

And it was Pank. Much broader, and therefore, by an optical illusion, much shorter; older and filled out; wearing a beard instead of being clean shaven; but Pank all the same. Pank, the active microbe, who in his lurid career at Felixstowe had bent many a Hun, and could always be relied upon to shake into activity even the most lethargic jellyfish. In an amazingly short space of time my empty glass was on the table before me, he had sucked out an outline sketch of my last ten years as though he were a large-bore semi-rotary bilge pump, found that I was thinking of returning to Canada, and had departed after saying

"You're coming with me in the *Swift*. New boat. Open your eyes. I'm running the U.S. Mail. It's two o'clock now; be at the White Line landing-stage at four o'clock. Hand-baggage only. One berth returned; lucky, wasn't it. Expect to be properly gouged for it. See you later."

Galvanised into activity by his breezy energy, I made more haste than I had for years, and was at the landing-stage at four o'clock. Here I found a motor-boat waiting, her sides covered with soft fenders, and when my scant hand-luggage was put on board we pushed off. As we rounded the dock I saw her in all her splendour, lying at a buoy in the harbour, the *Swift*, a great triplane flying-boat.

But such a boat. She was pure white hull, struts, and wings. Her six propellers seemed to be of some bright metal, for their curved surfaces caught the sun and winked points of fire at me. She loomed very large as we approached her, the top plane towering above us as we passed under her lower wing, but until the motor-boat came alongside her light steel hull I did not realise how big she was, so well was she proportioned. She was clean as a whistle, without a single excrescence, beautifully streamlined. The simplicity of the whole design was a revelation.

The man in the motor-boat told me that the soft fenders of his craft were to prevent his scratching the "anti-skin friction paint." I asked him what it was for. He was very vague, but thought it made her slip easily through the air, everything was covered with it, "wings and everything."

Climbing up a short companion-ladder and passing through a gangway, I was met by a steward who was apparently expecting me, as on giving my name he collected my hand-luggage without a word. He led me down a short alleyway. It opened into a long narrow dining-saloon, about twelve feet wide and forty feet long, set out with small tables and easy-chairs. There were a number of passengers fussing about and blocking the narrow space. As he led me aft I noticed that on each side of the saloon were five cabin doors.

At the end of the saloon we passed through a door in the middle into a rather narrow passage, which dipped down quickly to give head room under the main spar and three fat steel cylinders, which came through the wall on one side and passed out on the other. The floor of the passage rose again to the level of the smoking-room deck. On each side of the smoking-room were five cabins. The steward opened one of the doors.

"'Ere you are, sir," he said.

It was a small place, not larger than eight feet long by six feet wide, and containing two fixed bunks, one above the other. All the fittings were of Spartan simplicity and extremely light. It was lit from the ceiling. The steward showed me how to work the ventilators, because the glass ports were fixed and did not open.

"When in the hair we're 'ermetically sealed, so to speak," he explained.

On coming out of my cabin I was met by the Purser. "The Skipper telephoned and told me to look out for you," he said. I asked him what time we started. "We'll take the air about six o'clock," he replied, "unless the mails are delayed by the train wreck, a bad pile up on the main line." And he offered the observation that he considered railway travelling dangerous, now that all the mail trains had been speeded up because of the competition of aeroplanes. "The road beds and rails are too light to stand the racket," he explained.

In reply to questions, he continued "Our scheduled time is seventeen hours, but we usually do the three thousand miles in fifteen, and will land in New York at three in the morning. No, it's not nine hours; you see we go west with the sun.

"We always make the run at night. You can post a letter as late as four o'clock in London and have it on a desk in an office in New York at eight o'clock next morning. Coming back? We leave at eleven o'clock in the morning, and the mails are delivered in London by ten o'clock. Then there's little room on board, and nothing to do, and while passengers are sleeping they don't take up much space or move about. We have forty on board; you were lucky to get a passage. All men this time. We occasionally have ladies, but not often; they prefer the surface liner, because they can dance and have a good time."

And then he told me what my passage would cost. The amount rather shook me. I asked if many people travelled by air when they had to pay such rates.

"List always full up," he replied. "Speed of transport means longer life, and they don't mind paying for life. Most of the passengers are men in big business, famous surgeons, or international lawyers, and they actually make money by it. They like to finish a day's work in London, have a day and a half in New York, and be back to carry on the following day. They have got to sleep wherever they are, and might as well sleep on board. They tell me they sleep like the dead. I suppose the idea of doing anything at such speed lets down their nerves. There's one stock speculator crosses with us every two weeks; he says it's the only decent night's rest he gets.

"By the way, your passage-money includes dinner; the line sets out to do you tremendously well. There's only room for half the passengers in the dining-saloon at one time; but dinner is on for three hours, and you can dine early or late. You will only get a cup of tea and a piece of toast in the morning, and have breakfast on shore."

He explained he would have to leave me.

"The Skipper told me you are an old flying-boat man," he said, "and, if he was not on board, to introduce you to the Chief Engineer."

I followed the Purser forward through the smoking-room, and, by means of a side door, to the engine-room. I was introduced to the Chief. As was to be expected, he was a Scotchman Angus Munroe.

To him I opened my heart. I explained I was a poor Rip Van Winkle who had not seen a flying-boat or chewed on a figure for ten years, that I was bursting with curiosity, and in the sacred name of Pity to tell me the horsepower, weight, dimensions, and speed of his wonderful boat.

His long face cracked in a smile.

"Ay," he said. "The Skipper told me you learned him to fly in a bit boat weighing six tons."

He waved his hand at three long fat tubes running athwart ship overhead, from side to side of the boat, on a level with the lower wings.

"Turbines," he explained. "Thirty thousand horse. Steam. But vara likely ten years ago you peddled aboot with internal combustion fakements chattering, clattering, and onreliable. But yon's power for you silent, reliable, sweet, and done oop in a penny packet. Vara likely in your heathen islands ye never heard tell of Janes Fluid. We make steam wi' it instead of water. I could do wi' holding the patent. Condensing? That was the deeficulty. Great volumes of steam coming off at great velocity. But Janes Fluid and Toogoods condenser do the beesiness."

"One moment," I broke in. "Back in 1919 the destroyers of the 'flotilla leader' class had thirty-thousand horse turbines."

"Ay," said Munroe, "I've rattled roond in them."

"If I remember rightly, they were three hundred and fifty feet long and did thirty-five knots," I continued. "They carried two hundred and eighty tons of oil fuel. That was enough for eleven hours at full speed, or three hundred and eighty-five miles. That is, they used twenty-three tons of fuel an hour."

"Mon, your memory's fine," assented the Chief. "Ye'll well remember they could dae fifteen knots for aboot a hunder and sixty hours on the same fuel, using maybe less than twa tons an hour.

"But yon's better engines. The laddie that designed them did a wairkmanlike job. For an Englishman they're no sae dusty. But we're getting out a set on the Clyde that'll make him sit up.

"Fifteen tons of oil fuel an hour they eat developing full power. She steps along at three hunder knots. Forby we tank seventy tons, it's enough for four hours and a bit, and that'll be fourteen hundred miles. But the Skipper dinna drive her at that, thank the Lord, for the bed-plates are a bit light for my immediate liking. Twa hunder's our cruising speed. That takes only three tons an hour and gies us maybe four thousand six hunder miles."

He opened a door in a bulkhead and showed me a small room. It was very bare. There was a small bucket-seat, a row of levers and a board covered with indicators.

"Yon's whaur the fireman sits," explained the Chief. "He holds the steam at six hunder poonds preesure and superheated to four hunder and seventy degrees. That's aw there is tae it."

He poured into my entranced ears the way the steam was made. The fuel tanks were below the second deck. The oil was pumped up to hot pipes and vaporised, and was then blown under pressure from a row of nozzles upon the generator tubes. The Janes Fluid flashed into steam somewhere in the tube, nobody knew just where. It boiled at 20 degrees below water and the super-heating gave it a tremendous expansion.

"Boilers?" continued Munroe, in answer to a question. "We dinna have boilers to blow up and smash things to smithereens. The steam is made just as fast as we need it. It's as flexible as an auld glove. If a tube blaws out there's only a bit hiss and the body at the levers cuts it out. It shows on an indicator. Twa three years ago they put in a thermostat to automatically control the pressure and temperature, but the elements in the gadgets were always warping and ganging wrang, and hand control is certain.

"But it's no' like the auld times, when a trained engineer was an engineer. There's nae wairk tae be done. It's a drawing-room life. If anything gaes wrang, it's 'Mister Munroe, the shore engineers are coming aboord.'"

He unscrewed an engine-room hatch. It was beautifully fitted, so that not a crack would show on the hull when it was closed. We stood together, with our heads out, and could look fore and aft along the hull and out on the snowy expanse of the lower plane. Immediately behind the trailing edge of the lower wing were two streamlined funnels, protruding above the hull about a foot.

"She's twa hunder and forty feet from nose to tip of tail," Munroe told me. "She's licensed to weigh twa hunder tons when fully loaded. That's eleven and a half poonds a horsepower. Wing surface? Fifty-one thousand square feet. That's maybe loaded to eight pounds a square foot.

"Four hunder and fifty feet she measures from wing-tip to wing-tip. You'll notice there's no wires exposed. And you'll notice maybe that each wing-spar gets smaller as it goes out. That's the advantage of being big. Your small machine has a wing-spar big enough to take the greatest load all the way out. Vara wasteful. But we're deesigned with tapering wing-spars, steel girders they are, and so save weight and head resistance. Cost more? Vara likely, but consider the speed.

"Weight? Yell have played aboot with hunder-ton steel ten years ago, but we wairk with five-hunder-ton steel. Five times as light as aluminium for the same strength, it is.

"You're looking at the props. There's six of them, driven by shaft and gears, a smart job the laddie that cut them was nae fule. No engines out in the draught to make head reesistance. Murad steel they're made of, wood never stood up to the rain. Low speed, high efficiency, variable pitch, they are; absorbing five thousand horsepower each. I remember reading in an old report where a big expert said one propeller could only absorb twa thousand horse, but he was wrang.

"Getting off? I whack up the turbines with the blades of

the propellers neutral, and then shift them to the correct pitch, and she accelerates on the water from nothing to seventy knots in less than forty seconds. She takes to the air inside of three-quarters of a mile."

Here we were interrupted by the tinkle of a bell, and the Chief told me the Skipper was on board in his cabin. If I went forward through the saloon I would find the door on the right-hand side, below the control cockpit.

I found Pank in his cabin, a roomy and comfortable place.

"Mail will be on board in ten minutes," he said, "and we'll push off at six sharp. Come up to the control cockpit with me and see us take off. We'll yarn about everything at dinner."

I followed Pank up a few shallow steps into the control cockpit. I was all agog for marvels, and was rather disappointed. It was a small place completely covered in with glass, following the streamline shape of the hull. There was a padded basket-seat for the pilot and a control-wheel and yoke, very similar to what I remembered in the old boats. The whole affair looked inadequate to handle the huge machine.

"Remember Queenie's servo-motor?" Pank asked, noting the direction of my looks. "All the actual work of moving the control surfaces is done by an adaptation of his patent. The pilot has no strain on him at all, and yet has the feel of the machine."

Looking over the side, I saw a fast motor-launch racing towards us across the harbour, piled high with mail-bags, and in another moment the mail was being hoisted on board. A Quartermaster entered and settled himself down in the padded seat.

"When we start," Pank warned me, "lean up against the back bulkhead. We accelerate twice as quickly as a tube-train, and you may lose your balance." And then to the Quartermaster: "Switch on all control telephones." The Quartermaster shut down a switch, and Pank said in his ordinary voice: "Purser, are all the passengers seated? "

"All correct, sir," said the voice of the Purser at my elbow, and looking round I saw that it came from a large disk in the bulkhead.

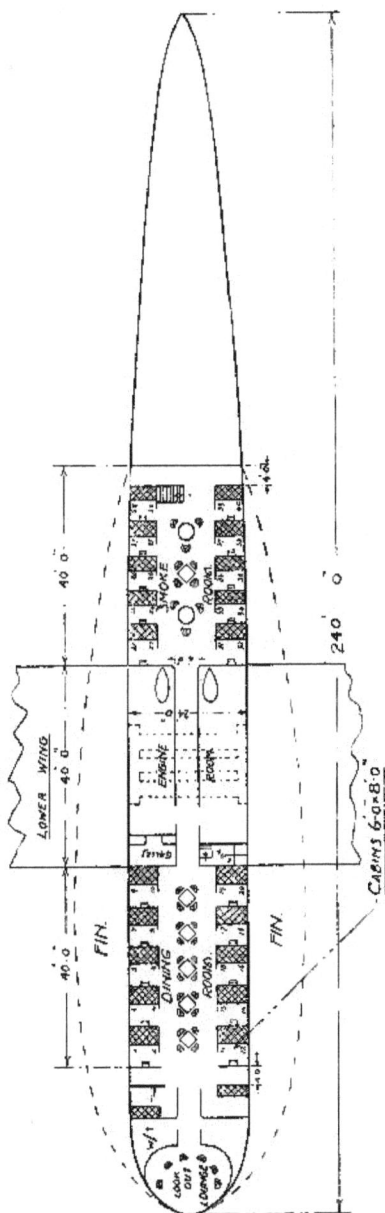

WHITE LINE
F.B "SWIFT" AND F.B "SWALLOW"
200 Tons.
SIX PROPELLERS - 30,000 H.P. LENGTH 240 FEET.
PLAN OF ACCOMMODATION.

CABIN DECK

SMOKE ROOM

ENGINE ROOM

DINING ROOM

LOWER WING

FIN.

FIN.

LOOK OUT

LOUNGE

CABINS 6'-0"×8'-0"

240'-0"

40'-0"
40'-0"
40'-0"

"Engines?"

"Engines started, sir," said the voice of Angus Munroe.

Looking back at the planes I saw that the propellers had vanished. There was a soft whirr, a soughing like a wind in trees, and a very slight tremor through the structure of the boat.

Pank looked at the row of indicators on the wall. All had a white disk down except in the spaces numbered two and three. "Seal doors two and three," he ordered. The two white disks dropped in the indicators.

"Bow-man, stand by to let go."

"Aye, aye, sir."

"Engines. Stand by for four seconds half blade on port propellers."

"Standing by, sir."

"Bow-man, let go."

"All gone, sir."

The tide carried us clear of the buoy.

"Engines."

The bow of the *Swift* swung round to starboard. She was heading for an open stretch of water.

"Quartermaster, ready. Engines, full."

I was pushed back against the bulkhead as though by a heavy hand as the boat leaped forward. The air speed indicator jumped to sixty knots, a hundred, a hundred and fifty, two hundred. There was no noise such as I had been accustomed to in a flying-boat. For an instant there had been the crash of a breaking bow wave, but now there was only a rubbing, rustling noise along the hull, and an increased soughing of the wind in the treetops. I learned afterwards that this noise was made by the oil vapour being forced through the nozzles in the generators.

"Level at six hundred," ordered Pank.

"Level, sir."

"Engines, two hundred knots."

"Twa-hunder, sir."

On a square ground-glass sheet in front of the Quartermaster appeared figures picked out in light.

"That's the wireless navigator," explained Pank. "He's on shore, but he keeps in touch with us all the way across. He gives us our latitude and longitude, the course to steer and the air speed to fly at. Simple, isn't it?"

All this time I had a dissolving view, a wild impressionistic sketch, of a sea snatched up in front of us and hurled behind. In six minutes, having travelled south, we were off Start Point, and the numbers on the wireless navigator, giving the course to steer, changed.

With a magnificent sweep of several miles and banking over slightly, the Quartermaster brought the *Swift* round on the new course and steadied. I noticed that he steered by a large gyro compass.

"No spill–all turns for us," laughed Pank. "No spins, or loops, or rolls."

At the height of six hundred feet our tremendous speed was apparent. The sea appeared to be working on a roller, pulled up over the horizon and passed back under us. Surface ships were in front, and then behind. In nine minutes we had the Eddystone abeam and in another ten minutes we passed the Lizard.

Every eighteen seconds, as steady as clockwork, a minute was added to the longitude on the wireless navigator, showing we had gone westward one mile. Every ninety seconds a minute was taken off the latitude, showing we had made a mile of southing.

Pank glanced at the figures.

"There's a beam wind of about twenty knots from the north," he said. "We are headed a bit north of our course to allow for the drift. It doesn't alter our speed though. The wireless navigator ashore has all the weather reports and adjusts our speed accordingly. With a following wind he usually slows us down to save oil, and speeds us up when we run into a head wind later on. Sometimes he shoves us through a region of high head wind at top speed. What we lose on the swings we pick up on the roundabout, and manage to get in on time."

"She's a bit nose heavy, sir," said the Quartermaster.

"Fireman, shift oil in forward tanks one and two," ordered Pank.

"When in the air," he explained, "we hold our fore-and-aft balance by an auxiliary elevator worked by a gyro through a servo-motor. But if the control surface has too much work to do it uses up power, so we shift oil fuel until we are in good trim."

I expressed amazement at the small amount of noise.

"Remember that small station that was working on silencing aeroplanes in 1918. It was washed out when the armistice was declared, but it had already laid the foundations for getting results."

Mr Wemp, the First Mate, came into the control cockpit, and Pank suggested I should look over the boat with him. He took me through her from bow to stern.

She had two decks.

The first deck ran from the bow to the leading edge of the wings, and from the trailing edge forty-five feet back. In the very bow, covered in with glass shaped to the streamline of the hull, was an observation cabin for passengers, containing six easy-chairs. Passing aft, there was the wireless room and captain's cabin on the starboard side, and the officers' cabin on the port side.

In the wireless cabin were two lads, one on duty and the other taking a busman's holiday. The latter showed me round. It all looked simple enough; the valves, amplifiers, coils, and gear were boxed in, and only the switches and plugs showed. The aerials were carried inside the wings. I had expected a great display of all the mysterious paraphernalia of the wireless wizard, but was disappointed.

I was shown the machine which sent out five dots every thirty seconds, so that the wireless navigator on shore could plot out the position of the boat.

"The old Morse system of signals has been washed out," the lad explained, "and if you wish to speak to anybody in England or America, we can plug you through on the wireless telephone."

Passing aft through the dining-saloon, with the ten double

cabins, I found the galley. Here a chef was already active at an electric range with aluminium utensils. The most delectable odours were floating about.

Then came the engine-room, and aft of this the smoke-room, and ten double cabins, with an alley-way running athwartship. We passed down a companion-ladder to the lower deck. This was a short deck, part in front of the engine-room and part behind. It had just sufficient accommodation for the crew.

"How many hands does this bus carry?" I asked.

"Eighteen in all, counting the five officers," the First Mate replied.

Then he took me down below and showed me the great oil-tanks, which were crowded as near to the centre of gravity as possible, under the engine-room. I took a look at the lattice-work steel keel which ran from the bow to the stern. It looked very light for the job it had to do.

From here I went forward to Pank's cabin, and when the First Mate had taken over in the control cockpit, Pank came down and asked, "Will you dine outside with the millionaires and suchlike, or shall we dine here?"

"Here," I replied, for I wanted him to talk.

After dinner, at his ease in an armchair, and prompted now and then by questions, he held forth.

"Remember in 1919," he began, "talking about a thirty thousand horsepower flying-boat. She could have been built then, even with the material and small engines available, but of course she would not have had the speed and carrying capacity the *Swift* has.

"In 1913, the Curtiss boat of sixty horsepower; in 1918, the Felixstowe Fury of eighteen hundred horsepower; in 1919, the first crossing of the Atlantic by a Curtiss-built American flying-boat; in 1923, the first ten thousand horsepower steam-turbine-boat; and now the thirty thousand horsepower boat.

"Remember the land-machine ramp at the end of the Great War; how they pranced on their hind legs and frothed about breaking the rails and shipping companies; and the blokes that

15-TON PORTE SUPER BABY, 1800 HORSEPOWER

put their good cash into companies that promised to carry mails and passengers by air over land and sea. What happened to 'em? Got into flat spins and crashed, mostly.

"Went into an optimistic company as a joystick merchant; saw the whole show from the inside. Tried to run mails in England. Weather conditions and the competitions of the railways did us down.

"Speed and reliability are the essence of mail-carrying. It's the time taken from the office boy licking the stamp until the presentation paper-knife slits open the envelope at the other end that counts, and the letter has always got to get there. The only letter-writers in a tremendous hurry, excepting the mad people who are frantically in love, are in the main centres of population, and they are connected by fast train services. Also, the wireless telephone rather put a bend in the show talk to anybody anywhere at any time.

"We had to have our aerodromes well out from the centre of the cities land too hard to get inside. Had to whiz the mail out from the post office to the bus, and tranship again at the other end. Took a lot of time. But the jolly old mail-trains started from a point near the post office, and the letters were sorted while the train was travelling. Mist or fog, gales and snow, blew our time-tables sky-high. You should have seen us tearing our hair in bad weather. Of course bad weather sometimes interfered with the train service a bit, but not to the same extent. There was nothing in it so far as time was concerned, and they had us beaten four ways on reliability.

"We speeded up the faithful old sky-wagons. But that meant bigger grounds to flop down into, so we had to go farther out from the cities. That made the time taken to get mails out to us a bit longer. We saved something at the receiving end by dropping the mails bang on top of the post office building. But the trains were speeded up too; they delivered special mails by motorcycle straight from the railway station. We had nothing on them.

"But with the increase of speed we had more crashes in fog and mist. Rain was troublesome too. Summer wasn't so bad, but winter put us down and out. Mails have got to be carried every day in the year. Important mails were delayed and sometimes destroyed. That fed up the men who wrote 'em. We tried putting up a kite-balloon above the mist, and gliding down from that. Not good enough. The aerodromes were too small, and the dashing aviators fetched up into houses, ditches, and trees. And, of course, a forced landing on the way under bad weather conditions was nearly always fatal. Insurance went higher than the machines.

"We weren't reliable enough. No commercial firm could stand the expense. The Government gave no assistance. The Treasury was squeezing every penny until Britannia squealed. We tried for two years, and then my little lot went *phut*.

"Yes, the mail-carriers had more success in less well-developed countries. Better weather conditions, longer runs, slower trains. But the money in it was nothing to write home about.

"Then passenger carrying.

"You remember the rather slow and clumsy four-engine aeroplanes they made such a fuss about? Well, they proved to be about the limit in size for a land-machine. Bigger ones were tried, but they were no go. Landing wheel loads, landing speeds, surfaces of aerodromes, big sheds, cost of crashes. The big slow aeroplanes could get into an aerodrome that the ordinary fast scout merchant could get down into, but when they speeded them up, so that they could get from one place to another in a thirty-knot wind in a reasonable time, they took the most of a county to land in.

"Then there was the weather. They had the same troubles as the mail-carriers and a few more. Pilots were paid to take risks, but passengers objected to being strewn over the countryside in a mixed lot of metal and matchwood. Fly on half-power plant? Not when fully loaded. Passengers didn't like to go above three thousand feet, it made some of them ill. Couldn't sleep after being up high. With heavy low clouds the aeroplanes had to go under them or over them. Below them, often at five hundred feet, it was too dangerous over land, chimneys, and houses on hills; and they couldn't get down any place like we can at sea.

"The only run that would have paid was from London to Paris, joy-riders mostly, where you had to change from rail to boat and back to rail again. But the Channel Tunnel and the cutthroat competition between aeroplane companies left nothing in the bag.

"Yes, like the mail-carriers, they did a bit better in places with decent climates, but the shareholders could never afford to travel by air on the dividends paid.

"Everybody all at once got wise to the fact that it was the long hauls over the water routes that were going to pay. Competitors, comparatively slow steamers, fifteen to twenty-five knots. One or two flying-boat companies had been working on the job and were not making such a bad fist at it. But the land-machine people had a cut at it. Couldn't get it into their heads that big flying-boats were just as efficient as big land-machines, and a bit faster, as they hadn't to carry landing wheels and undercarriage.

"What happened? They drowned a good many people, lost a lot of mails and machines, and gave it up after about two years of bitter experience. You see they were handicapped by having to land on aerodromes in mist and fog, and couldn't get up to the same speed as flying-boats.

"The airship people?

"They are not doing badly, but they're essentially fair-weather craft. I don't mean mist and fog, for they can hover with engines shut down, but wind.

"The two million cubic foot gas-bags produced in 1919—by the way, the Germans had 'em that size at the end of 1917 had only a top speed of sixty-seven knots when new. Head resistance and skin friction. Their cruising speed was something like forty-five knots. They found there was only about eighty days in the year they could cross the Atlantic with safety, and they had to go south-about through the anti-cyclonic weather. Their average time was three days, not much better than a five-day surface boat. But they did carry on.

"They stuck to the job and built ten million cubic foot gas-bags top speed eighty-three knots. They were really too slow for Transatlantic work. They were very very costly, and as they carried big loads the companies had a hard time getting enough mails and passengers to pay for operating them. Safe enough, much safer than travelling by surface ships, but too dependent on the wind. Speed is what counts.

"In the meantime the big armament firms and steamship companies were sitting on the fence, watching the other fellows spending money and buying experience. They experimented a bit and gathered a lot of valuable data. One of the steamship companies had flying decks put on their liners, and when within three hundred miles of harbour launched mail-carrying aeroplanes. It cut down the time tremendously.

"Flying-boats?

"Not much was done with them. The Air Ministry was starved for money, and big boats were too costly for small firms to play with. Fortunately some bright blokes in the Navy had experiments carried out in their own yards. Somehow, even in the hardest of hard times after the Great War, the Navy managed to get money. I suppose they knew that trouble was coming.

"Remember the drawings of the fifty-ton flying-boat we looked at in 1919? Well, that was built, and proved more or less of a success. It was found that a boat of that size could be built of steel, so the steel merchants were got busy and finally succeeded in making two-hundred-ton steel, and eventually got to five-hundred. It was a costly business.

"There was really nothing screamingly successful until the ten thousand horsepower turbine came along. Janes Fluid made them possible for aircraft. Ordinary steam made from water is full of air, and that makes condensing difficult: air-pumps and so on. Ammonia was tried a long time ago and other true fluids, but the mechanical difficulties were too great. Then Janes struck on a true fluid that answered the purpose.

"And then came war.

"You don't want to hear about it? Well, we had a Labour Government, and the Army and the Air Force became less than

Erecting the 15-ton Felixstowe Fury

nothing, and the Navy was rather down at the heel, and the Empire was on the verge of breaking up. So a pushing Island People made a snatch at Australia and the islands in the Pacific. The League of Nations? That for practical purposes was the British Empire and America, and the enemy tackled both. Fortunately our Navy had about twenty ten-thousand horsepower flying-boats. I joined up at once and saw the only fleet action.

"Remember the comic Russian with the aerial torpedo they were experimenting with in 1917? Right idea, but wrong principle. Wouldn't work. The gunnery sharks took the idea, pulled it about, worried it, and produced the flying bomb. I believe Sperry tried it in 1915. They produced ton bombs with wings. Each boat carried two.

"We ran into the enemy in force. While the warships were piling on the heavy stuff we unloaded from ten thousand feet. The bombs glided a mile and a half for every thousand feet we were up. They were balanced by a gyroscope and steered by wireless. We nose-dived them into the lightly protected decks and made rather a wreck of the enemy. What was left of him was bottled up in his ports.

"Then we went after them. We'd let go from twenty miles out and the bombs would sail over boom and harbour defences. The surface ships had no chance. When we were finished you could have bought the Navies of the world for a song.

"The enemy was a stiff-necked and brave people, so we had to smash up a few of his coast towns before he surrendered. Aeroplanes? They hadn't got our speed, and if they had got at us we could have settled them with our one-inch quick-firers before they could have got close enough to get home. Anti-aircraft guns? We always unloaded too far away for them to touch us. You see, we didn't have to pass over the target.

"And that was what put flying-boats on their feet. The whole of the British Navy is now in the air. It's a fine sight to see a destroyer flotilla.

"The bigger the boats got, the faster they were. Scale effect. Streamline 'em better and save weight in the hull. No trouble getting off or on, there's lots of water. Fog? No more dangerous to us than it is to surface ships. The Wireless Navigator tells us where we are to within a mile. And if the fog is very thick in a harbour, or the clouds are right down to the water, we land outside and taxi in, just as we used to do.

"Remember Queenie's night-landing gadget? It put a boat down on the water automatically. You let a lever hang down over the side, shut off your engines, glided down, and when the tip of the lever touched the water it pulled back the controls and the boat landed smoothly. We use an adaptation of the gadget today.

"Cost? You may be surprised to know that our two boats running the U.S. Mail just pay their way and no more even with the Government subsidy. Our company runs smaller boats, ten thousand horsepower, down through the Mediterranean, to Australia, and in various places all over the world. They pay, but the big ones don't make money yet. They will in time.

"And now let us yarn about the old days."

So we yarned about Felixstowe, and the six-ton boats, and the pilots, until he had to go to the control cockpit to relieve the First Mate.

"Like to come up before you turn in?" he asked.

We went up together. It was pitch dark outside. The control cockpit was lit only by the light in the binnacle and the Wireless Navigator.

"What happens about looking out from your glass-house when it rains or snows?" I asked.

"At our speed rain and snow won't stick to the streamlined glass," he replied. And then to the Quartermaster, a new man, for the first one had been relieved: "Put me through to the *Swallow*."

When the Quartermaster shut down a switch, he said, "Hullo, Morrison. Going strong. What's your position?"

A rich jovial voice at my elbow answered: "Good evening, Pank. Have you come for the ashes?" This was evidently some obscure joke, for the two Skippers laughed heartily together.

And Pank asked: "How's the Missis and kids?" Then Morrison gave his position.

"That's our sister ship, east-bound," Pank said to me. "Keep a sharp look-out over our port bow and you'll see her lights. She'll pass in a moment."

I looked out into the darkness and caught a momentary glimpse of a bright white light and a red one. They were gone in a flash.

"That's her," said Pank.

I went below to my cabin and turned in. The next thing I remembered was a steward standing at my elbow with a cup of tea.

"Where are we now?" I asked.

"We'll land in twenty minutes," he replied.

I scrambled into my clothes and went up into the control cockpit, where I found Pank. The daylight was just beginning to creep over the water.

"On time to the minute," said the Skipper.

"There's the Statue of Liberty," I cried.

And then Pank: "Quartermaster, stand by. Engines, stand by. Engines, cut off."

We glided down towards the grey water silently and flattened out. I felt the great wings cushioning as we ran along above the surface. We touched. The sharp keel began to drag the speed down. There was the roar of a breaking bow wave. And then she settled in and stopped.

"Bow-man, smart with the line," ordered Pank, as a motor-launch ran across our bows. We were in tow. "Unseal doors two, four, five, and six," he continued. The disks in the indicator were lifted.

Looking across the harbour I saw a mail-boat boiling towards us and an oiler standing by to pass us a filling hose when we were made fast to the buoy. Another motor-boat was on its way out to collect the passengers.

"I thought that crossing the Atlantic in a flying-boat was going to be an adventure," I said.

"Not at all," replied Pank. "It's a business."

www.ingramcontent.com/pod-product-compliance
Lightning Source LLC
Chambersburg PA
CBHW021101090426
42738CB00006B/443